THE OVERFLOW
BLESSING

FROM REVELATION TO MANIFESTATION

BY ANDRE BRIGHT

THE OVERFLOW BLESSING BY ANDRE BRIGHT
Published by: Mad Praise Music Publishing

ISBN: 978-1-7331779-0-0
Copyright © 2019 by Andre Bright
Cover design by: Freeman Multimedia Bluebird Digital
Interior design by: Damonza.com

Available in print or e-book on Amazon.

For more information on this book and the author visit: Andre Pierre
Bright or Mad Praise Music Publishing on Facebook.

Scripture quotations are taken from the HOLY BIBLE NEW INTERNATIONAL
VERSION r. NIVr Copyright c 1973, 1978, 1984 by International Bible Society.
Used by permission of Zondervan Publishing House. All rights reserved.

Scripture quotations from The Authorized (King James) Version. Rights in the
Authorized Version in the United Kingdom are vested in the Crown. Reproduced
by permission of the Crown's patentee, Cambridge University Press.
Scripture quotations taken from the New King James Version®. Copyright ©
1982 by Thomas Nelson, Inc. Used by permission. All rights reserved.

Library of Congress Cataloging-in-Publication Data
Bright, Andre
The Overflow Blessing / Andre Bright 1st ed.

Printed in the United States of America

CONTENTS

INTRODUCTION

YEARS AGO, I received a series of prophetic words that resonated in my spirit and provoked me into action. Years later, it looked as if my life was headed in the direction diametrically opposed to what had been prophesied. Looking for answers, I turned to the Word of God to understand why everything in my life seemed contrary to what had been spoken over me. During my quiet time, the story of Joseph leaped off the pages at me. Here was a Bible character who must have felt many of the things I was feeling.

By chance, are you also like Joseph? Have you have received wonderful, mind-blowing prophecies but have yet to experience the manifestation? Or maybe a prophetic dream or vision resonated in your spirit. Maybe you feel you have taken a step of faith and launched out into the deep, doing the things God told you to do, but have yet to receive the promised harvest. Your flesh wonders why things are not happening. The vision seems so far away. You are asking questions like, *God, why did you close that door where everything was good? Why am I out here struggling in this wilderness season?* If any of these statements ring true, you are not alone, and this book is for you.

The prophetic word or dream is often associated with a blessing God has in store for His people. Now, this is no ordinary blessing. This is an *overflow blessing,* which is described in Malachi 3:10. One that will require stretching your tent in order to receive it. God has a process for preparing believers to receive this special blessing.

This process will require leaving the comfortable place where you know how to do everything. It will require moving into an unfamiliar area and experiencing challenges that will prepare you. This is a place where you as a believer will learn the power of obedience, the importance of managing emotions, and how to expand your skillset. Knowing the steps behind the overflow blessing will enable you to understand where you are and how you are going to achieve your destiny. Between the revelation of destiny and the manifestation, there is a period of time which God uses to prepare the recipient for the next level of blessing. Could it be He is wanting to do the same in you? Rest assured, at the appropriate time, God will open a door that no man can close and elevate you into a new season.

We can see the elements of this process in the biblical story of Joseph. Like you, Joseph received a vision from God concerning his future. He embarked on a thirteen-year roller-coaster journey of highs and lows before the door opened for him to walk into his destiny. If you are familiar with the story, have you ever wondered how he endured those dark days? How was he able to have favor wherever he was placed? How was he so positive and successful? How did he forgive the treachery of his brothers? These questions prompted me to launch a personal study that ultimately culminated in this book. Now, writing a book was not on my list of things to do in life, so God had to nudge me onto the path of authorship.

In 2012, He closed the door on my work in the corporate world. As a faith walker, I expected a new door to be opened shortly to allow me to continue my lifestyle. But God had other plans, and I wandered in the wilderness for several years before I had the right perspective to write this story. During that time, the Lord dealt with me about disobedience, pride, emotional swings, strategic positioning, isolation, and elevation. I learned a lot about love, forgiveness, gratitude, speaking, life, and humility. These were painful lessons, and one might argue that I was a slow learner. In hindsight, I can see how each test, setback, obstacle, and closed door had a purpose in shaping my character and teaching me to crucify my flesh. At the right time, God faithfully redeemed all those experiences to manifest His will for my life. He will do the same thing for you.

In going through this process, I began to understand why many believers struggle to achieve their destiny. It grieves my heart to think how many people have aborted the preparation process designed to bless them. They struggled to trust God during difficult times, because they have chosen their will over God's will. Consequently, they leave the path God had for them and wander in the wilderness until they die. This is sad because the Bible says *many are the afflictions of the righteous, but the Lord delivereth him out them all* (Psalm 34:19 KJV). In order to see the deliverance of God, we have to experience some struggles that are beyond our ability to resolve. Why do we become so agitated with God and want to abort the process? For me, it was due to my lack of knowledge. Thankfully, studying the story of Joseph encouraged me to walk faithfully into my new season.

My wilderness experience taught me wonderful lessons about the God we serve. I learned to trust Him with things that are precious to me, and He was faithful to redeem my sacrifices. He refined my character, purged my iniquities, pruned my abilities, and increased my capacity to love. In doing so, He prepared me to receive what He had in store for me. Looking back, the turning point for me occurred when I became totally dependent on God for everything. Now, my desire is to enlighten believers about the process God uses to prepare us for our destiny.

My hope is that this book will encourage you to endure the preparation process and emerge victorious with the promises of God. Journey with me as we uncover the process God uses to prepare us to receive our overflow blessing.

CHAPTER ONE

The Overflow Blessing

Bring the whole tithe into the storehouse, that there may be food in my house. "Test me in this," says the Lord Almighty, "and see if I will not throw open the floodgates of heaven and pour out so much blessing that there will not be room enough to store it."

—Malachi 3:10 NIV

DO YOU REALIZE what God has placed inside you? He has blessed you with wonderful gifts and talents to enable you to achieve your destiny. Granted, they are in seed form and will require cultivation and development. But when they blossom and mature under the trials of life, you will experience what author Rick Warren describes as a purpose-driven life. Living life on purpose brings contentment and fulfillment, because you are completing what you were designed to do.

Hidden inside you is your kingdom assignment, otherwise known as your destiny. God hid the survival of Israel in a Hebrew slave who never lost faith despite all the difficulties he faced. God hid the deliverer of His people in a basket floating on the Nile river. God hid the seeds of a nation in the loins of a liar and a cheat. God hid a fierce warrior inside of a timid and frightened farmer. God hid a giant-killer in an outcast young boy tending sheep in a distant pasture. Now, imagine what God is hiding in you. What is God's plan for your life?

The story of Joseph serves as an excellent illustration of how God's plan unfolds in our lives. The story begins in Genesis chapter thirty-seven where God revealed Joseph's future in two separate dreams, followed by a series of trials that tested Joseph's faith and his trust in the Lord.

First, Joseph lost his freedom, then he was falsely accused of attempted rape and thrown into prison. Finally, he was forgotten by the very people he had helped. But through it all, God used each challenge to prepare and position Joseph to have an encounter with the most powerful man of that age. When Joseph finally interpreted Pharaoh's dreams, he stepped into the future God had revealed to him. What he stepped into was the *overflow blessing*.

I believe there are some key lessons we can learn from studying the story of Joseph, lessons that will enable us to achieve our God-inspired destiny. Every negative occurrence that happened in Joseph's life had a purpose. Each one served to reposition him, to prepare his gifts, to mature him, and to protect him. At the appointed time, Joseph was ready to not only interpret Pharaoh's dreams but also solve Egypt's pending problems. God positioned Joseph so that Pharaoh could see the exceptional wisdom and knowledge of this young man. When Pharaoh hired Joseph, he became the second most powerful man in Egypt. His story illustrates the process one will experience on the way to the overflow blessing.

The Overflow Blessing

What is the *overflow blessing*? Through the prophet Malachi, God describes a blessing of tremendous proportions available to those who are obedient to His commands.

Bring ye all the tithes into the storehouse that there may be meat in mine house, and prove me now herewith, saith the Lord of hosts, if I will not open you the windows of heaven and pour you out a blessing that there shall not be room enough to receive it.
—Malachi 3:10 KJV

Simply stated, the overflow blessing exceeds man's ability to imagine, comprehend, or orchestrate. It is so incredible it confounds human logic. The only plausible explanation for such a blessing must acknowledge the existence of a Being far superior to mankind. For the believer, we know this being to be God, our Father. The stories of the Bible confirm the infinite power and authority of God. All things in both the natural realm and the spiritual realm bow down and worship Him. We serve the God of the impossible—nothing is too hard for Him.

The overflow blessing cannot be consumed by the generation that receives it. Instead, it leaves a legacy of blessings for several generations. The residual of the blessing spans many years. With proper stewardship, it can significantly increase in value. The Bible contains examples of people who received this type of blessing. Abraham, Jacob, Joseph, and David all benefitted as well as their children and their grandchildren. Their stories have blessed believers for thousands of years. Even 21st century readers have been blessed by their stories of faithfully serving an incredible God.

The blessing we're studying is a God-ordained, God-sanctioned, and God-orchestrated event. Getting into position to receive this blessing will require faith, perseverance, long-suffering, and growth. Specifically, we will have to endure a process designed to refine our character, increase our faith, and prepare our gifts/talents. It will require obediently following the leading of the Holy Spirit. It will require moving out of the comfortable place and walking in unfamiliar territories. It will require letting go of things and people in order to move down the path toward what God has prepared for us.

Finally, it will require the ability to subject our will to the will of the Father concerning our lives, which is really a mindset transformation.

In Isaiah chapter fifty-four, the prophet wrote about the Lord who redeems and restores. In verse two, he talks to the Israelites about increasing the size of their tents in anticipation of a move of God. He proceeds to prophesy about the mighty things God will do for the nation. The symbolism of the tent is so powerful, because it speaks to increasing one's capacity to contain and to store. For those who will enlarge their tents, they are able to receive more from God. For the modern-day believer, the tent can represent many things ranging from our mindset, to our abilities and talents, to our level of faith, or our willingness to grow. The one thing that is clear is God's blessing will require personal change and movement in many areas of our lives. When I started this journey, I thought I was ready for my own overflow blessing. In retrospect, that was my arrogance trying to shortcut the transformation process. Thankfully, the process resulted in me finding my purpose and making me a better individual. I know it will do the same for you.

Has God given you a vision or dream that seems impossible to achieve? Does He periodically send reminders of who you are in His eyes (e.g. through prophetic words of encouragement from people who do not even know you)? Do you sense greatness in your life despite the circumstances? Do you have an uneasiness with where you are in life? Do you feel there is something great you are supposed to do? If you answered in the affirmative to any of these questions, you are a candidate to receive an overflow blessing from God.

The story of Joseph provides believers with an opportunity to study this type of blessing. God took the tragic situation of Joseph being sold into slavery and worked it out for the good of two nations. This life-altering event put in motion a plan that would ultimately bless Joseph and his entire family.

Have you experienced a life-altering event that made you question God? For me, it was my divorce. It started me down a path very similar to what Joseph experienced. What about you? Have you been falsely accused by people? Have you been punished for things you did not do? Have you been forced to relocate or change jobs? Have you been overlooked for opportunities despite being overly qualified? Have recent life events caused you to question whether you are in the will of God? If so, do not despair, and do not give up hope. In the midst of the madness, our sovereign God has a plan. Like Joseph, you will eventually prosper at a new level. The key is recognizing that you are in God's transformation process. This process will train you to receive an overflow blessing.

Receiving the Overflow Blessing

There are some key characteristics all successful candidates for this blessing possess. They have faith in God and know that through Him, they can do all things. They believe God is sovereign in their lives. This means God has complete control over everything that happens to them. They have the ability to hear His voice and obey His instructions. Finally, they are willing to excel in every situation they find themselves in. If this is you, you are a candidate for God's greatest blessing.

Receiving this type of blessing will require significant changes in our lives. Our character must be tempered to minimize flaws that would cause the blessing to overtake us. We will be strategically positioned to meet key people and have critical discussions. We will also take opportunities to develop and perfect our gifts and talents. In order for all of this to happen, we must:

- Be able to move by faith.
- Be obedient to the Word of God.
- Be comfortable allowing God to direct the steps in our life.
- Believe He has a plan to prosper us and not to harm us, regardless of how things look or feel.

- Conquer our emotions and gain control of our mouth.

- Trust God in every situation we find ourselves in. This can be quite challenging when the Enemy is blasting us with seeds of doubt and discord.

Like Joseph, we must be careful who we communicate our vision to. The Enemy is watching and will do everything he can to discourage us. His goal is to poison our mind with negative thoughts until we give up on our vision. He's quite shifty in his craft, and nothing is too low for him. That's why he uses the people around us to accomplish this objective and compel us to cast aside our vision.

That's why it is important to use discretion when sharing your vision with people. I am sure the slaves in Potiphar's house could have cared less about Joseph's dream. From their perspective, Joseph was a slave just like them. And he was never going to be anything other than that. I imagine the prisoners mocked Joseph when he was thrown in the king's prison for attacking Potiphar's wife. *Sure, you are innocent. Why else would you be in jail with us?* I wonder what they thought upon hearing Joseph had been placed in charge of all Pharaoh's affairs?

Unfortunately, people without a vision will kill ours prematurely. Hopeless people show disdain for those who are excited about their future. Jealous people fiercely criticize those they perceive to have a larger vision. And fearful people will attempt to poison those who are moving by faith. Insecure people spend so much time worrying about other people's perceptions, they will second-guess their vision and stop moving toward it. Therefore, it is imperative to use caution when sharing our vision. We should never value the opinions of man over God's.

Do Not Forfeit Your Blessing

When faced with trials and adversity, many people forfeit their blessing because they stop pressing forward. One study found that 90 percent of people who failed once, simply quit trying altogether. But successful people are ones who learned from failures and refused to quit. The journey to the promised blessing will be filled with challenges designed to stretch and train us. We will experience difficult times due to the Master gardener pruning us to produce much fruit. But the key to our success can be found in trusting the process.

Unfortunately, in our season of preparation, we can become discouraged by negative opinions from friends and family. Instead of allowing God to fight our battles, we retaliate against people who have treated us poorly. Instead of excelling in every situation, we may choose to perform poorly because we feel slighted or overlooked. Instead of rejoicing in the sovereign nature of God, we might choose to complain and murmur about our current situation. Instead of embracing our circumstances, we covet the blessings of others. Instead of accepting change, we fear moving out of the comfortable place. We struggle to forgive and are always lamenting about the past.

The latter was one of the major reasons the Israelites were sentenced to wander in the desert and die. They constantly made their challenges out to be bigger than their God. They allowed the same spirit of fear which kept them in slavery to convince them to reject the promised land. No wonder so many believers have given up without receiving what God had for them. Let's examine three factors that cause people to stop moving toward their blessing.

Pride, distractions, and disobedience cause many people to forfeit their overflow blessing. Pride resulted in Gehazi being cursed with leprosy. Instead of receiving the mantel of Elisha, his name was never mentioned again in the Bible. Distractions cause many people to settle for a "good thing" and miss out on the "great thing" of God. Ahab allowed his marriage to Jezebel to distract him. Under her influence, the nation reverted from worshipping Yahweh to worshipping the god of the Phoenicians. Similarly, disobedience caused Saul to lose his kingdom. He was more worried about pleasing the people than being obedient to God.

Pride

Pride will cause us to grab the vision and run toward it *independent* of God. Instead of allowing God to order our steps, pride will cause us to move out in our carnal knowledge. Before we realize it, we will have spent money and time on things that are struggling to produce fruit. Soon, we find ourselves not making progress despite doing everything we know to do. Despite working harder, it seems we are moving backward.

Finally, when setbacks and disappointments cause our frustration to peak, our pride rises up and aborts the process. And we ask, *Why did God give me a vision, then not allow me to achieve it?* This is where the Enemy plants those seeds of doubt that will cause the immature to question their faith. Unfortunately, many have fallen away because of this reason.

Pride will cause us to abandon the season of preparation. It screams that we are ready to receive the blessing *now*! Pride will cause us to elevate the carnal man over our spirit man. This results in believing we can achieve the vision without God. This is a very dangerous place for believers.

The Bible says, *God opposes the proud, but shows favor to the humble* (James 4:6 NIV). Why the humble? Because they have endured God's transformation process, and the Fruit of the Spirit is evident in everything they do. The humble acknowledge God as both Lord and Savior. Their desire is to walk down the path God has for their lives. The humble naturally give all glory and honor to God. For them, being approved by God takes precedence over being seen by man. We will cover the power of humility in a later chapter.

Distractions

Distractions are anything that takes our focus away from God's plan for our life. The Enemy loves to bring distractions and counterfeits across the believer's path to distract us from our God-given vision. Over time, distractions will cause us to stop advancing toward the vision. It will cause us to settle on the goodness of man rather than the greatness of God.

Distraction can come in many shapes and forms. Sometimes the distraction is a relationship. At times it is a job paying more money, which may take us away from the one God appointed us to for a season and reason. Sometimes it is immediate recognition versus staying in the obscure place where God has us. At other times it is the constant allure of social media. One thing is certain, the Enemy wants us to lose sight of our vision. Distraction will cause us to surrender our future blessings in return for today's pleasures.

Disobedience

Disobedience is extremely dangerous for believers, because it will take us out of the will of God. Rejecting His commands will highlight areas in our lives that are not surrendered to Christ. Consistently choosing our carnal knowledge (meager in size) over the infinite wisdom of God shows we have not allowed Him to be sovereign in our lives.

Saul disobeyed Samuel by offering a burnt sacrifice to God for favor in attacking the Philistines. When Samuel found out, he told Saul his kingdom was not going to endure because of his disobedience. The Bible says, *the Lord has sought out a man after his own heart and appointed him ruler of his people because you have not kept the Lord's command* (1Samuel 13:14 NIV). If Saul had waited on Samuel to arrive, the Lord would have established His kingdom over Israel for all time. But Saul chose to worry about the opinion of man versus being obedient to God. Because of his disobedience, Saul forfeited the overflow blessing.

Don't allow disobedience to disqualify you from your blessing.

It's Not God's Fault

At this point, you may be asking why so few people experience an overflow blessing? The answer can be found in the parable of the wedding banquet in Matthew chapter twenty-two. Here, Jesus compares the kingdom of heaven to a king having a wedding banquet. He describes how many people rejected the king's invitation because they were busy with the cares of life. He goes on to point out how others were denied access because they did not come dressed for the event. Jesus used this parable to explain how the Jews would reject Him and how the same invitation would be presented to the Gentiles. In Matthew 22:14, Jesus said, *for many are called, but few are chosen* (KJV). This begs the question, why are few chosen?

The simple answer is that many people fail to answer the call or they come unprepared. In the parable, Jesus mentioned the one man who was turned away for failing to wear the proper attire. The wedding clothes symbolize the preparation required to enter the kingdom of heaven. Many are excluded because they did not prepare themselves in advance. The same principle applies to the overflow blessing. Many people are called to receive this blessing, but few are willing to complete the preparation process. Because they choose to abort the process, they disqualify themselves from receiving.

One of the saddest examples of missing the overflow blessing can be found in the story of the Exodus. Despite God's tangible presence, the Israelites chose to rebel against Him. Never mind that God led them out of Egypt with a pillar of cloud by day and a pillar of fire by night. Never mind that He performed many miraculous signs on the way to the promised land. When the people received the negative report of the ten spies, they rebelled against God and cried to return to Egypt. In response, the God of the Israelites condemned them to wander in the desert for forty years until that fearful generation died out. The writer of the book of Hebrews used their story to warn about the consequences of disobedience. Hebrews 3:7-11 says:

So, as the Holy Spirit says:

Today, if you hear his voice and do not harden your hearts as you did in the rebellion, during the time of testing in the wilderness, where your ancestors tested and tried me, though for forty years they saw what I did. That is why I was angry with that generation. I said, "Their hearts are always going astray, and they have not known my ways. So, I declare on oath in my anger 'They shall never enter my rest.'" (NIV)

As I said, that generation of Hebrews forfeited the blessing. Don't allow the same thing to happen to you. When you hear His voice, don't hesitant to obey. Prolonged disobedience will open the door for a judgement absent of grace and mercy.

Qualifying the Called

Now that we understand what the overflow blessing is, let's look at the process God uses to prepare us to receive it. First, He will reveal our future using dreams, visions, or prophetic words. Then He will use life experiences to move us outside of our comfort zone in a place that is foreign to us. In this wilderness place, He will allow us to be strategically positioned, prepared, and stretched.

During this season, we will be in training to develop our character, strengthen our skills and experiences, walk in humility, and control our emotions. Once we have made significant progress in all of those areas, He will elevate us to receive the overflow blessing. He is faithful to redeem and restore all we have experienced so we may be a living testimony of His grace and mercy.

Do you have what it takes to obtain an overflow blessing? I believe you possess the capability to claim your own promised land.

Summary

Writing this book helped me understand how God has directed my steps to walk in a greater blessing. All of the things that have happened in my life were designed to train me and increase my capacity to receive from God. As I reflect on past events, I recognize that everything had purpose. I can see His hand guiding and positioning me during times I felt alone and abandoned. Each situation taught me to trust Him and to stand on His Word. For that, I am eternally grateful. Clearly, God prepared me to receive my overflow blessing. Now, I have the opportunity to share with you what I have learned in my journey.

We serve a loving Father who desires the best for His children. Why? Because it reflects the nature of His goodness. He knows how He made us, what gifts were placed inside of us, and the purpose for which we were designed. God has a specific path for each of us that leads to an overflow blessing. One that glorifies the gracious nature of God. One that highlights His tender mercies renewed each day. One that reminds people nothing is too hard for our God. One that tells unbelievers of how great our God is.

If you are confused and frustrated concerning your current situation relative to God's promises over your life, do not despair. Journey with me as we learn about the process God uses to prepare us for our destiny. Do not be discouraged by the situation you are in. You are being positioned and trained to receive a blessing.

But let me warn you in advance. You will need to stretch your mindset to receive this information. This book will require the reader to confront pride, self- perceptions, selfishness, arrogance, and insecurity. It will inspire you to change your attitude, increase your gratitude, and strengthen your fortitude. You will begin to understand there is a purpose behind every hardship and setback. Everything happens according to the master plan God has for your life. In reading this book, my prayer is that you will see God's hand moving in a tangible way in your life.

Looking back on the past fifteen years, I am grateful for the many lessons I have learned going through this process. I now have the opportunity to share some key principles that will enable you to achieve your blessing. The Bible says God's people are destroyed by a lack of knowledge (Hosea 4:6). So, stop guessing about your purpose or your destiny. Draw closer to the One who created you, and let Him order your steps. I invite you to walk with me as we study the path to the overflow blessing.

Reflection Questions

1. When did you make Jesus Lord of your life?

2. How often do you seek God's will for your life?

3. When was the last time you asked God to order your steps?

4. How is your current attitude helping or hindering your destiny? What changes do you need to make in order to continue progressing toward your destiny?

5. Have you experienced times when your pride caused you to be distracted? How did you get back on track?

Meditation Scriptures

Jeremiah 29:11
Romans 8:28
Proverbs 16:9
Proverbs 16:18

CHAPTER TWO

God's Love for Us

For I am convinced that neither death nor life, neither angels nor demons, neither the present nor the future, nor any powers, neither height nor depth, nor anything else in all creation, will be able to separate us from the love of God that is in Christ Jesus our Lord.

—Romans 8:38-39 NIV

ONE DAY IN 2017, I had a long conversation with my youngest daughter about some difficult topics. Initially, she was hesitant to ask me a question because of how I might respond. When she told me about her hesitancy, a thousand negative thoughts rushed through my mind. I quickly brushed them aside as I assured her of two things. First, I told her she may not like my opinion on the subject or the answer to the question. Then I reminded her that despite our differences of opinion, I would always love her.

She smiled and proceeded to ask her question, and we talked for over two hours on topics such as LGBT issues, abortion, immigration, racism, legislating morality, and the fact that people did not know Obamacare and the Affordable Health Care Act were one and the same. While she did not like some of my responses, she realized nothing was going to change the fact that she was my daughter, and I would always love her no matter what.

Thinking about that conversation reminds me how much our heavenly Father loves us. The Bible says in Genesis 1:27 that God *created mankind in his own image* (NIV). God is our ultimate father, and we carry His seed in us. And He is such a good father. He loves us despite our flaws, sins, shortcomings, and failures. He is faithful and steadfast in His love. As a loving parent, God wants to prepare us to receive the blessing He desires to bestow on his children. He wants to direct our steps and provide provisions as we walk out our destiny. Yes, God is a good father who wants the best for his children.

A Fathers Love

The Bible tells us nothing can separate us from the love of God (Romans 8:38). God loves us despite our rebellious nature and waits patiently for His children to return back to Him, because His love is unconditional. The Bible defines love as being patient, kind, non-envious, non-boastful, and refusing to keep a record of wrong doing (1 Corinthians 13:4).

God was patient with me when I was running from my calling. God gave me grace and mercy when I was judging others. God loved me when I was buried under the weight of poor life decisions and sin. When I finally reached the end of my strength, He was there waiting for me. He received me with loving arms and reminded me I was His child. Indeed, God is love.

Let's put this into perspective. Ask yourself this question: *Is there anything that would stop me from loving my children?* For me, I realize nothing could ever stop me from loving my children. Not their poor choices or holding ideological differences from me. Not unhealthy relationships or committing crimes against humanity. Not wearing ugly fashions and rooting for the wrong college team (go N.C. State

Wolfpack). I will always love my children. Just like my parents loved me and their parents loved them. It was unconditional, unwavering, and unlimited.

Don't get me wrong, I may not like my children's decisions or actions. And yes, I understand there can be serious consequences to our actions, because the Bible teaches that a man will reap what he sows (Galatians 6:7). Let me be fully transparent. My mother did not like some of my choices, and she was very vocal about it. She was quick to share her displeasure every time I saw her, but she was faithful in her love. So is the love of God.

But here is the amazing part about God's love for us. God sent His only Son to the earth to be a perfect sacrifice for the sins of mankind. Jesus left His place in heaven to be born into a sinful world. During His thirty-three years on earth, He endured hardships, trials, disappointments, joy, sadness, and persecution. He experienced everything you and I struggle with today before He took his position on the cross to be crucified for our sins.

This is where it gets real. Can you imagine sending one of your children to die for anyone? It was difficult for me to even write the question much less think about it. *No way!* I would die for them, but not expect it to be the other way around. This is how much God loves us. He sent His only Son to be the perfect sacrificial lamb for you and me. Even the angels marvel at God's love for mankind. Instead of sending the death angel to destroy sinful mankind, God sent a perfect Lamb to save the world. Simply put, His love is amazing.

Receiving His Love

Chapter four of 1 John emphatically states that God is unequivocally love. But that is not what I heard while growing up. I remember hearing about God judging sinners and sending them straight to hell. I felt like if I did anything bad in the church, God would strike me down with judgment.

Pastors of that day held tent revivals and preached damnation for all who failed to repent of their sin. With all the fire and brimstone messages—and none on love and grace—I grew up scared to death of God. I prayed to Him for good grades and successful job interviews, knowing He did not approve of my carnal lifestyle. At that time, I convinced myself love was on the other end of the spectrum from where God resided. Boy, was I wrong.

Although christened as a baby, I ran from God for many years before finally accepting Jesus as my Savior in 1999. As I became a committed church-goer, things started happening as I changed. My marriage improved. One Sunday, the message convicted me about my cursing, and I prayed for deliverance. Deliverance came quickly, which encouraged me to surrender other areas of my life. The Lord was faithful to His Word, and I experienced fruit in these areas. Unfortunately, my pride would not allow me to fully surrender other areas to the Lord.

Eight years into my newfound faith walk, I found myself in a different situation. For one, that great marriage I talked about earlier was hurtling toward the finish line. I destroyed the love my spouse once had for me. In my quest to be *right*, I failed to operate in love. After being married for twenty-one years, I had to learn how to live by myself again. That alone broke me. Though I continued to experience some success on my job, I felt like a total failure, completely worthless on a personal level.

While my circumstances were bad, to say the least, something good did come out of that horrible time in my life. Some friends told me about a church with a dynamic young pastor. I decided to visit Raleigh North Christian Center one Sunday in November of 2006. There, I experienced the overwhelming love of the Father. The praise team was singing "Living Word" by Fred Hammond. When the song started, tears ran down my face. I began to weep. My weeping morphed into deep, painful, uncontrollable sobs that emanated from a place of disappointment, frustration, anger, and embarrassment. As

I released those emotions, I felt the love of God in a way I had never experienced. When I was at my worst, He met me and embraced me with His loving arms. It was then I experienced the agape love of our King, Jesus Christ.

Over the next several years, my personal relationship with the Lord grew. He healed my emotional wounds, dealt with my disappointments, confronted my sins, increased my trust in Him, strengthened my faith, and redeemed my dreams. In retrospect, I can see how God was preparing me for an overflow blessing.

Looking back, I can see all the key signs: *positioning, preparation, training, elevation,* and finally, *redemption.* The failures and hurts caused me to move to strategic places. The subsequent challenges cleansed me of old hurts and bad habits. The monthly tests helped me to get God's Word deep in my heart where I could ultimately trust Him.

Slowly, my behavior changed. My response to life challenges aligned more with the Word. I found that as I deliberately put my will to death, God reminded me of the plans He had for me all along. In time, He elevated me to a redemptive place personally and financially. After sowing faithfully for years, I began to reap a harvest of incredible proportions. I am so grateful because, in retrospect, God's plans were so much better than anything I could desire or imagine. That is why I can say with assurance God loves us.

On that fateful day in 2006, I experienced an outpouring of God's love that changed my perspective of the One who created me. My brokenness was nothing for Him to heal. My sins were easily cleansed by His blood. He embraced the brokenness. When He did, I realized He was, indeed, love. Then the reality hit me, His love is pure. It has the power to redeem, to heal, and to restore.

Later, a study of 1 John uncovered a truth I had never seen before. It is a hard teaching, so brace yourself, as it may apply to you. I learned that anyone who does not love, does not know God. It's that simple. *No love, no God. Know love, know God.*

By trade I am an engineer who was trained to believe there is a logical explanation for everything. Given that God is love, my brain struggled to understand why bad things happened to me. Like most of you reading this book, I could not help wondering why He would allow things to happen to the child He loves. The answers did not come easily, but I was blessed to be in a teaching church that increased my knowledge of the Bible.

I learned that some bad things are simply the consequences of our actions and words. Thank God for His grace and mercy. At times bad things happen because God is not welcome in a particular environment, region, or nation. Sometimes bad things happen to get us on the path God has for us (e.g. Joseph thrown in the well). Sometimes He allows things to happen in order to position people to do His will (e.g. Moses). In order to accomplish His plan, God will allow things to happen that cause us to embrace His will for our lives.

But God will never come against our free will. He will not make us love Him. He wants us to make a decision to love Him because of who He is. Things happen in our lives based on our own decisions, actions, and words. Consequently, we will have the opportunity to draw closer to Him or reject Him. The choice is ours alone. When we surrender our will and accept His will for us, He promises to guide our footsteps and make our path straight. We express our love of the Father when we choose to follow His Word and His guidance.

What are your actions telling God today?

Reaping What We Sow

The Bible says a man will reap what he sows, and we know that a seed will always produce after its own kind. Orange seeds produce orange trees, and apple seeds produce apple trees. In the same way, when we sow good things, we will reap a harvest of good things in due season. Contrarily, when we sow bad things, we will reap a harvest of bad things. Even from this principle of sowing and reaping,

God will not come against our free will, no matter how loving He is. We reap what we sow. It is a natural law *and* a spiritual law.

Some years ago, my pastor taught for several weeks on the consequences of our actions. Using various Scriptures, he established the connection between our thoughts, beliefs, actions, and the consequences. In emphasizing the power of our words, he highlighted the connection between our negative thoughts and negative things coming into our lives. He also pointed out that when we speak positive things, we reap positive outcomes.

Our words and actions reflect what is truly in our hearts. The Bible says that *as he* (a man) *thinketh in his heart, so is he* (Proverbs 23:7 KJV). The Bible also says that the heart of man is *desperately wicked* (Jeremiah 17:9 KJV). The pastor explained that because Adam brought sin into the world, mankind will always have the propensity to sin. But Jesus came and died on the cross so we can be reconciled unto God by His redemptive blood. Man is no longer a slave to sin. No longer do we have to bring blood sacrifices, and no longer are we separated from God by our sin. Jesus paid the price so we can approach the throne of God with confidence.

The Bible says *death and life are in the power of the tongue* (Proverbs 18:21 KJV). So, over the next several years, I deliberately became cognizant of the connection between the things that happened in my life and the words I had spoken. Keep in mind, I have always had a critical eye in that I tend to notice every imperfection rather than what is good. Admittedly, my words were often very critical, which had an impact on my interactions with others and how I perceived most everything. I was convicted in my spirit many days for unwarranted criticism, but I failed to make a change.

Finally, in 2013, I made a decision that significantly changed my life. I decided to only speak positive words that uplifted and encouraged people. I would only use words that promoted wonderful possibilities and a bright future. Slowly, I saw changes in my life.

More importantly, people recognized a profound difference in me. Gone was the critical, know-it-all, I-told-you-so Andre.

Additionally, during this period of reflection, I noticed there were times when bad things should have happened, but they didn't. That's when I realized God's mercy was on my life. Other times, I saw where I received favor in terms of appointments and prominent assignments. I am convinced that was because of His grace and favor on my life.

In this context, grace is defined as the free, unmerited favor of God. It means to get things you did not earn. For example, grace is when you receive favorable raises and bonuses even though you may receive an average performance rating.

Mercy means compassion or forbearance, leniency. It means to not receive what you deserve (judgement). Mercy is when you receive a warning ticket, though you were caught traveling fifteen miles above the posted speed limit.

What type of fruit are your words producing?

God Has a Plan

God loves His children, and He desires that we have life abundantly. He has plans for our lives, *plans to prosper you and not harm you, plans to give you hope and a future* (Jeremiah 29:11 NIV). I love this Scripture, because the prophet is talking to the Hebrew remnant living in exile.

Jerusalem had been invaded and captured by the Babylonian army of King Nebuchadnezzar. Many of the captives were taken back to Babylon and were now living under foreign rule in a foreign land. This all happened against the backdrop of the Lord Himself saying that *He caused* them to be carried away from Jerusalem (because of their disobedience and idolatry). Despite their captivity, He instructed them to build houses and plant gardens in this foreign land and to go on living prosperous lives. The Lord told them they would live in exile for seventy years, but He shared this encouraging word with them about the plans (that were still in play) He had for them despite their circumstances.

Notice how the plans involved actions that would make them prosper and give them hope. Do you think it is interesting—as I do—that the Lord told them His plans for captivity would not harm them? By implication, that bit about the prospect of harm coming their way indicated there would be some challenges along the journey to reestablishment as an independent nation. No matter how daunting they may have seemed, the challenges would not bring harm to God's people.

When modern day believers face challenges as we walk out our respective destiny, we are reassured that God is in control, and His plans will not harm us. Nevertheless, they may require some periods of being uncomfortable as we walk toward the prosperous blessing God has ordered for us.

God reveals his plan for our lives through dreams, visions, and prophetic words. This revelation serves as the focal point as we traverse the landscape of life to achieve our destiny. In the story of Joseph, God gave the young man a dream that revealed part of the plan He had for Joseph's life.

Joseph dreamed that his brothers were binding sheaves in the field, and his own sheaf arose and stood upright, while his brothers' sheaves stood round about and bowed to Joseph's sheaf. When he shared this with his brothers, they became very angry, because the symbolism of the bowing suggested Joseph was going to rule over them.

Later, Joseph had a second dream that he told his brothers and his father. In that dream, the sun and the moon and the eleven stars bowed down to him. This time, his father Jacob rebuked Joseph for implying that his mother and father would bow down to him. But God had a plan for Joseph that would ultimately save his family from annihilation and create the twelve tribes of Israel as we know them today. Notice that God confirmed His Word via the second dream, but understanding the meaning of the dream would require Joseph to embark on a thirteen-year journey. I will discuss this more in later chapters.

Once God gives us a revelation concerning our destiny, He orchestrates activities that move us outside of our comfortable place. As uncomfortable as things become, God's promise remains the same. He will lead those who are willing to hear his voice and obey his commands. Here is the difficult part: trusting God as you walk according to His instructions without being able to see the path to the end result.

According to Christian author Stormie Omartian, God only gives us enough light for the step we are on. She wrote that with each step of faith, He will reveal the next step to take. But again, only after the first step is taken. The King James Bible says in Psalm 37:23, *the steps of a good man are ordered by the Lord: and he delighteth in his way.* God does not want to see us stumble through life. He promises to lead us and make our crooked paths straight—if we allow Him to do so. As we allow Jesus to be both Lord and Savior, we put into motion the things God wanted for us in the first place. God is so faithful to His Word. Read what He says about guiding us:

> *Trust in the Lord with all your heart and lean not on your own understanding; in all your ways submit to him and he will make your paths straight.*
> —Proverbs 3:5-6 NIV

To allow God to direct our steps, we need to trust that He has a plan for us. That trust has to transcend all seasons—the good and bad. His plan is working for us even in the most difficult of times. But this is where we must stand on His Word. Romans 8:28 says that *in all things God works for the good of those who love Him, who have been called according to His purpose* (NIV). It took me a few years to fully grasp this Scripture. First, I had to accept that God was sovereign in my life and that Jesus was my Lord. I then had to understand free will and the consequences of my actions. Finally, I had to understand that the Enemy can only do what God allows.

Can you see how this is starting to make sense? God's plan is to prosper us and not to bring us harm. Walking out God's plan involves doing things we have never done and going places we have never been. In order to be obedient, we must be able to move past our level of understanding and submit ourselves to His direction. As we trust Him in the uncomfortable place, He works on our behalf to prepare us and position us for a greater blessing.

Because He will *never* come against our free will, we must voluntarily submit to His leadership. We must make a choice to allow Jesus to be both our Lord and Savior. Unfortunately, many people call Him Savior, but few call Him Lord. When we submit to Him as Lord, we acknowledge that He has total control over our lives. It means we have surrendered our soulish desires to receive God's desires. When we do this, we become a branch of His vine, with God as the vine keeper (John 15:4-7). As His will becomes our will, and our thoughts align with His Word, we begin to see the manifestation of His promises. Soon, we are walking on the path that leads to our destiny. This was God's desire from the beginning. God has a plan, and He loves us.

Summary

Looking back over my life, I realize God took me through a process to train and prepare me for a greater blessing. He loves me so much that He would not give me the blessing prematurely, because it would have overwhelmed me. He guided me down a pathway to prepare me for walking in my destiny.

In retrospect, the difficult times were not punishment, they were preparation. They were meant to purge me of character flaws and wrong beliefs. They were designed to get me to move to the right place. They were designed for me to develop knowledge, perfect my skills, and gain wisdom. Finally, they were purposeful to help me understand and walk in the Word of God. He understood my destiny and lovingly prepared me for it. God is a good father.

Understanding God's love for us is crucial to grasping the deep revelations that are buried in the story of Joseph. Wayne Corderio, the author of *The Divine Mentor* wrote that we can study the lives of individuals in the Bible to gain wisdom and understanding on how to deal with challenges in our own lves. For me, the story of Joseph aligns with my personal experiences and likely to those of many believers. It speaks to a process God uses to take us from the revelation to the manifestation of His blessing. Joseph's story gives us insights into the purpose of vision, positioning, preparation, and elevation. He has placed a desire in my heart to share this with you.

Now that we know God loves us, let's delve into the process that prepares us to receive the overflow blessing. The things you are experiencing are part of His plan. The challenges and tests all have purpose. And they will not overtake you. The story of Joseph illustrates the process God uses to prepare believers to receive the overflow blessing.

Over the next several chapters, we will explore this process. Know that God loves you. He desires to direct your path across the wilderness to your promised land. Are you ready to follow him?

Reflection Questions

1. Describe the first time you experienced God's love.

2. How has God shown His love for you?

3. What are the consequences of sin?

4. How have you been blessed by God's grace and mercy?

Meditation Scriptures

Deuteronomy 7:9
Psalm 86:15
John 3:16
Romans 5:8
Ephesians 2:4-5
1 John 4:7-8

CHAPTER THREE

Vision Defines the Destination

And the Lord answered me, and said, "Write the vision and make it plain upon tables that he may run that readeth it."
—Habakkuk 2:2 KJV

BEFORE WE KNEW Him, God knew us. He carefully crafted each of us to achieve the plan He has for our lives. We were born with a unique set of gifts and talents to achieve our destiny. Every step in our life has shaped and molded us to a point where we can fulfill our purpose. The challenge is understanding the purpose for which we were created. Finding our purpose will require spending time with our Creator to understand the assignment He has specifically for us. Once we have this understanding, we can align our actions to achieve our divine destiny.

The way we see life impacts the way we live. Our perspective determines where we invest our time, energy, and resources. People who operate with a clear vision utilize resources effectively to achieve their destiny. They understand their purpose, and there is a sense of deep satisfaction in moving toward it. On the other hand, people without a clear vision will squander their resources, chasing everything and accomplishing nothing. Their lives are filled with frustration from not accomplishing what they were designed to do.

The success of Rick Warren's book *The Purpose Driven Life* highlights the fact that many people go through life without understanding their God-given purpose. When I read that book, I was one of those people searching for my purpose. God has a plan for our lives, and He will equip us to excel and prosper.

God desires to reveal to His children the vision for their lives. He accomplishes this by sharing this information through dreams, open visions, and prophetic words. It is incumbent upon the receiver to acknowledge the information and do something with it. For those who can receive the revelation, they make this revelation the goal which drives all their actions. The challenge is to walk each step by faith in order to bring about the manifestation of the vision.

The overflow blessing always starts with a revelation from God. He will communicate a glimpse of the end state to prepare us for the journey. The Bible says that *the Lord confides in those who fear Him; He makes his covenant known to them* (Psalm 25:14 NIV). The word *covenant* means an oath-bound promise between different parties. God's covenants always speak of things to come.

God's revelation will always seem impossible to achieve given our current state. It will require significant growth on our part: in our character, our relationship with Christ, and our knowledge base. Refusing to change will cause us to miss out on God's plan for our lives. Imagine the emptiness of working your entire life without achieving your divine purpose. Sadly, many people have gone to the grave with regret and unfulfilled dreams.

What has God revealed to you about your purpose and destiny?

The Power of Vision

Vision is defined as having the ability to think about or plan the future with imagination or wisdom. It is the art of seeing what can be before it exists. It requires one to see what cannot be seen by our natural eyes. Vision:

- Inspires action and invokes passion.

- Establishes direction and defines purpose.

- Provides motivation to do things that haven't been done before.

- Attracts money and resources.

- Creates focus and synergy.

- Enables ordinary people to achieve extraordinary results.

- Justifies sacrifices and suffering for a season.

- Empowers growth and change.

- Fuels tenacity, perseverance, and decisive decision-making.

- Determines destiny.

- Inspired the Wright brothers to learn to fly.

- Inspired Alexander Graham Bell to invent the telephone.

- Drove Martin Cooper to invent the cellular mobile telephone.

Are you willing to chase your God-given vision in order to achieve your destiny? There is tremendous power in having a clear vision. Studies have shown that organizations with clear vision tend to accomplish great things. It allows them to focus their energy and resources on doing a few things exceptionally well.

BMW and Audi excel at making high-performance luxury cars. Apple excels at smart phones and computers. The Becton Dickenson and Stryker Corporation excels at high-quality medical devices. All these companies utilize their unique vision to minimize distractions, ensure goal/resource alignment, prioritize activities, and drive time-sensitive results. Businesses that lack clear vision tend to be a "jack of all trades but master of none." Their legacy is marked by missed opportunities and average performance. History confirms that people and organizations that operate with a clear vision of their future enjoy exceptional success. "The poorest person in the world is a person without a dream" (Dr. Myles Monroe).

Receiving the Vision

God will often reveal His intentions before He makes a move in the earth. Amos 3:7 says, *Surely the Sovereign Lord does nothing without revealing His plan to His servants the prophets* (NIV). He does this so people will recognize His hand at work. When things happen in God's timing and in His manner, everything will point back to the source: God. Those who heard His voice before they saw the work of His hands will have their faith and confidence in Him strengthened. Their testimony will bring glory and honor to God.

It takes faith to receive the vision God has for us. When an angel spoke to Gideon while he was threshing wheat in a wine press, he called him a mighty warrior. But Gideon could not receive what the angel said. He responded that his clan was the weakest in Manasseh, and he was the weakest in his family (Judges 6:15). It took several miraculous signs to convince Gideon to step past his fears and into his destiny. But once Gideon grasped the vision, he went on to lead his people in victory over their enemies in battle.

What will it take for you to receive God's vision for your life?

The Bible is filled with people whose lives were impacted by God-given dreams and visions. God told Abram his descendants would be enslaved for 400 years before being delivered to walk in prosperity. Joseph and Daniel interpreted dreams for the leaders of great nations. Solomon received wisdom from God in a dream. Dreams directed Joseph to take Mary for his wife and later to take the baby

Jesus and flee to Egypt. Even Saul complained to the witch that God had stopped speaking to him in dreams and visions.

Dr. Joe Ibojie defines the difference between a dream and a vision in his book *The Illustrated Dictionary of Dream Symbols*. He says a dream always occurs in the unconscious state of our sleep. A vision is an image of revelation or supernatural occurrence that takes place while the mind is fully awake. Dreams often contain symbols that reveal the deep things of God. They tend to be more like parables, which require the Holy Spirit to decipher them. In contrast, visions contain great clarity and seldom require interpretation. While each communication channel functions in uniquely different ways, they can both be used by God for sending a personal message.

The question is what has God revealed about your destiny? Has He spoken to you in a recurring dream? Has he given you visions or prophetic words? Do you have the faith to receive what He revealed to you?

Unfortunately, many believers struggle with this because they do not recognize the importance of dreams and visions. That is why it is important to maintain a journal to capture dreams, visions, and prophecies. It is the job of the Holy Spirit to decode the message and provide understanding and clarity.

Acts 2:17-18 summarizes the importance of believers being diligent with journaling:

In the last days, God says, I will pour out my spirit on all people. Your sons and daughter will prophesy, your young men will see visions, and your old men will dream dreams. Even on my servants, both men and women, I will pour out my Spirit in those days, and they will prophesy. (NIV)

It is imperative that believers draw from their dreams, visions, and prophecies to understand God's desire for their lives. For those of us who can relate to Gideon, God will send a confirmation of His Word so we don't have to guess. But in order to understand His plan, we must be willing to walk out of the comfortable place by faith. As we begin to move, the vision becomes our destination. Our God promises to order the steps of the righteous so we don't have to guess about direction. The manifestation will occur when our actions, thinking, and sacrifices come together to achieve the goal God has for us.

If you are wondering about your purpose or lack of a vision, seek out the Father's face and allow Him to reveal the plan for your life.

Vision Gives You a Destination

Dr. Steven Covey emphasizes the importance of having a vision in his groundbreaking bestseller, *The 7 Habits of Highly Effective People.* He introduces the concept of *Begin with the End in Mind,* which discusses the power of visualization. In his study of highly successful people, he found a strong correlation between having a clear picture of the future state and successful outcomes.

Stated differently, if you can see it, you can achieve it. A vision gives you clarity on where to focus your energies and actions. It gives you a target to continue striving for when you are in the midst of uncomfortable situations that test your faith and your patience. Dr. Covey encourages setting goals that align with the vision and reviewing them weekly to stay on course and minimize the potential for being distracted. Knowing where you are going helps you understand where you are and what you need to do next.

In the story of Joseph, God utilized dreams to reveal the plan he had for saving the seed of Abram and birthing the nation of Israel. The manifestation of Joseph's dreams set in motion actions that would ultimately fulfill the prophecy God gave Abram (read Genesis 15:1-4).

Joseph had a dream, and when he told it to his brothers, they hated him all the more. He said to them, "Listen to this dream I had. We were binding sheaves of grain out in the field when suddenly my sheaf rose and stood upright while your sheaves gathered around mine and bowed down to it."

—Genesis 37:5-7 NIV

Shortly after the first dream, Joseph had a second dream, which he shared with his brothers and his father. In Genesis 37:9 it says that in his dream, the sun and the moon and the eleven stars bowed down to him. His father quickly rebuked him and sarcastically asked if Joseph's family would bow down to him. God revealed Joseph's future at an early age despite his inability to understand the importance of dreams. Interestingly, his family rejected the dreams and failed to comprehend their significance.

But God had a plan. Time eventually revealed that the bowing symbols represented Joseph's authority over nations and kings. With the fulfillment of the dream, God released an overflow blessing that benefited Joseph's family for several generations. Out of their descendants would come the twelve tribes that formed the nation of Israel.

Joseph clung to that dream over the next thirteen years while God prepared him for his destiny. He did not give up while he was in shackles on his way to Egypt. He returned good for evil while working in Potiphar's house. He was faithful in his responsibilities while he was imprisoned in Pharaoh's jail. Neither of these places aligned with the dream God gave him. But Joseph was able to set his sights far above his circumstances. I believe he knew slavery was not the end state for him. Nor was prison his final destination.

Joseph maintained his focus on God's promise through the trials, setbacks, and disappointments. Instead of lamenting on the past, he concentrated on making the best of his immediate situation, because he knew it was temporary.

Fast forward. God wants to do the same thing for His people.

The situation you are in today is temporary. God desires to take you higher. Have you grasped the vision God has for your life? What are you laboring to achieve?

Vision Creates Unity

Having a clear vision is critical for unifying people and getting them engaged. The story of Nehemiah provides an excellent illustration of this point. Nehemiah had a vision for rebuilding the walls around Jerusalem. They had been torn down and burned when the city was conquered by the Babylonians. God heard Nehemiah's prayers and granted him favor with King Artaxerxes. Armed with letters for safe passage and provision, he returned to Jerusalem to engage the remnant in rebuilding the wall around the city. But Nehemiah faced a huge challenge when he returned to Jerusalem.

The inhabitants had grown accustomed to living in the heavily damaged city. They were disillusioned and content to live in a state of despair. More importantly, they lost sight of God and the fact they were His chosen people. Nehemiah addressed this negative perception by challenging them to rebuild the wall in order not to be an embarrassment to God (Nehemiah 2:17). The people responded to Nehemiah's leadership, and they organized themselves to complete the task at hand. By working around the clock, they completed the wall in fifty-two days.

Nehemiah's vision attracted resources from King Artaxerxes. His passion for the vision rallied the people in the city to embrace the vision, take decisive action, and make sacrifices to rebuild the wall. His strong leadership skills enabled them to achieve tasks his enemies thought to be impossible. There is power in a well-articulated vision.

In 1994, Corning Inc. made the decision to compete for the Malcolm Baldridge National Quality award again. The executive leadership team formulated a vision and rolled it out to the senior leadership of the Telecommunications Products Division (TPD). The vision quickly rolled down into the 1995 performance objectives for all TPD employees. The leadership team did a great job of engaging people and building enthusiasm for the challenge. Soon, there was a new level of synergy in the business unit as everyone aligned their personal actions with the overall objectives for the division. It was clear that winning this award would require sacrifices by the entire organization.

While a focused team worked on preparing Corning's story for the submission, TPD continued to provide high levels of service to their customers while ramping up capacity and implementing new products. The organization's commitment to excellence could be seen in customer satisfaction reports, customer service metrics, quality metrics, financial performance, retention rates, and associate morale. This concerted effort resulted in the division being selected as a finalist for a site visit. With the vision in reach, people from all pay levels rallied to be able to articulate the success story. The Malcolm Baldridge site assessment team was impressed by the unity and focus of the 1800 people in the division. They awarded Corning the prestigious honor in 1995. Yes indeed, a strong vision will unify ordinary people to do extraordinary things.

Vision Creates Action

Once people understand the vision, they can support it with actions that will bring about the manifestation. We can see this point exemplified in the construction industry. Before a builder can start a project, he must have a set of blueprints to tell him what to do. These plans provide the builder with a detailed vision of what will be built and how it will be built. They contain pictures of the building at different stages of construction and all the pertinent details such as materials, construction methods, and critical dimensions.

Once the builder has the blueprints, he can now direct people working on the project. The site construction manager will utilize the plans to develop a construction schedule, coordinate material deliveries, and forecast resource needs. Construction workers will take the plans and complete their individual tasks under the watchful eye of the site manager. Over the course of several months, the site goes from uncleared land to a complete multi-office building.

Vision creates a bias for action. When I was young, my father would always say my brother and I would be the fourth generation of college graduates in my family. He continued to speak that over our lives for many years until he saw the manifestation. William Andrew Bright had a vision for his children. He wanted the best for us, and he understood the power of education. As a good father, he sowed in faith to prepare us to achieve that vision.

Many years later when I had children, I told them early on they would be the fifth generation to graduate from college. They hated hearing me say that, because it felt like I was putting pressure on them. But in reality, I was imparting a vision of their future that was tied to the family's legacy of education. Now that they have achieved this milestone, they understand the importance of both the vision and the legacy behind it. I suspect they will say the same thing to their own children.

Guard Your Vision

Once you receive the revelation for your life, you need to be careful who you share this information with. Unfortunately, not everyone desires to see others be successful. If you share with the wrong people, you will open yourself to being hurt by those who cannot embrace where you are heading. Joseph's brothers could not see past the livestock in the fields. They could not foretell the famine that was going to grip the land or how God was going to position and elevate Joseph to solve Pharaoh's problems. Instead, they criticized and mocked their brother and, in their anger, sought to harm him.

Let's be clear, people criticize what they don't understand. Those with big visions can only be understood by others with big visions. Over the years, I have heard several sermons on the difference between eagles and chickens. Eagles represent people with God-inspired visions who are destined to achieve great things. They can be characterized by having faith that is stronger than their fears. They are motivated by achievements and are always looking to go higher.

On the other hand, chickens represent people whose fears are stronger than their faith. Even though they may receive a God-inspired vision, they choose to remain where they are. They prefer stability over change and are reluctant to try new things. The following quote summarizes the difference between chickens and eagles. "No one can consent to creep when he feels the impulse to soar" (Helen Keller).

Over time, I have observed some interesting dynamics between the two. Eagles view challenges as opportunities to make a difference. When a vision is shared with an eagle, they will encourage you to soar higher. They will often share success stories to motivate others and are willing to support your ascension.

In contrast, chickens view challenges as problems which they would rather avoid. Chickens shun change and are comfortable in the status quo. When someone shares a vision that will cause them to leave the comfortable place, they will point out all the reasons not to pursue the vision. They will convince you that things are lovely where you are. Their goal is to talk you out of pursuing the vision. That's why it is imperative to use discretion when sharing your vision. "People seldom improve when they have no other model but themselves to copy" (Oliver Goldsmith).

Let's talk about naysayers for a moment. These are the people who are comfortable with the status quo. Their narrow perspective limits them from seeing the benefit in new ideas and inventions.

Imagine the opposition Columbus must have experienced when he was trying to gather support for his expedition to the new land. The predominate thought of that time was that the earth was flat.

Many people did not want to invest, because they thought Columbus would fall off the earth if he sailed too far.

History is full of examples of people rejecting the new thing. Horse-carriage makers failed to see the potential of a motor car. IBM scoffed at personal computers. Blockbuster ignored Netflix. Retail giants overlooked Amazon Prime. Don't let naysayers drown out your vision. Continue pressing forward to fulfill your destiny.

Starting the Journey

Once we have a vision for our destiny, many of us will rush out and start working toward it. Instead of seeking God's direction, we will begin constructing a direct path to the destination. All is well until we experience a series of obstacles that cause us to pause and question if we really heard God.

Andy Stanley wrote in his book *Visioneering* that "a divine vision is dependent on God making it happen." Simply put, they are impossible to achieve without Him. Jesus explained this to the disciples when He taught on the vine and the branches. *I am the vine, you are the branches; he who abides in Me and I in him, he bears much fruit, for apart from Me, you can do nothing* (John 15:5 NIV).

When we try to manifest the vision in our own strength, we make a horrible mess. Since we were bought with a price, we no longer have the right to apply our gifts and talents to things outside the Father's will. Instead, Proverbs 3:5-6, instructs us to trust in the Lord and not to lean on our own understanding. When we acknowledge Him in all our ways, He promises to make our paths straight.

For me, I have learned to seek God's face immediately after receiving a dream, vision, or prophecy. Though I may start several activities and knock on different doors, I will only proceed down a path once I receive a confirmation. Once I started doing this consistently, my frustration level decreased significantly as I stopped wasting energy going down so many dead-end streets.

Summary

God created each of us to achieve a unique purpose. In order to live fulfilled lives, we must understand our purpose and make it our vision. There is nothing more frustrating than to work your entire life only to feel empty and incomplete because you failed to walk in your divine purpose.

Thankfully, God is faithful to communicate a vision for our lives via a variety of methods. But it is ultimately up to us to align ourselves with God's plan. We must accept His plan and then embark on the journey to achieve it. A God-inspired vision cannot be achieved without having a relationship with Him. We must depend on God's guidance and provision to achieve our destiny.

God gave Joseph a dream concerning his future. I believe Joseph made that dream his vision, and it helped him navigate the difficult times of enslavement and imprisonment. God strategically positioned Joseph to one day become the second most powerful man in Egypt. During the time between the delivery of the dream and the manifestation, God taught Joseph to trust Him explicitly. The many trials served to shape Joseph's character and humble the impetuous youth. Because Joseph humbled himself to God's will, God exalted Joseph in His perfect timing to receive the overflow blessing. He wants to do the same thing for you.

Just like Joseph, God gave me a vision. Then He put things in motion in my life that, on the surface, appeared to move me away from that vision. Looking back, I realize He was preparing me to receive the blessing He had for me. I learned to recite Romans 8:28 over every circumstance in my life, because that Scripture reminded me how every obstacle, every rejection, every setback, every disappointment happened for a purpose. I learned to ask God what I was supposed to learn from each situation. Because of the revelation God gave me for my life, I knew He was preparing me for something great. Finally, I learned to encourage myself by reciting God's promises. *You are never given a dream without being given the power to make it true* (Richard Bach).

What has God revealed about your purpose? Have you reflected on the prophetic words that have been spoken over you? For those who have had reoccurring dreams and visions, have you inquired of God for more understanding? If you are unsure of your purpose, ask your heavenly Father to reveal it. Once you receive it, surrender to God, and allow Him to lead your life. He knows the right path that will take you to your destiny.

Once we understand our purpose, the next step is leaving the familiar place and traveling in unfamiliar places. Just remember, you are not alone. God will help you achieve the purpose He created you for.

So, let's begin our journey.

Reflection Points:

1. What has God revealed to you about your destiny?

2. Do you have your vision posted someplace where you can look at it every day?

3. Have you experienced any distractions? If so, how have they impacted you progressing towards your vision?

4. Who is speaking life over your vision? Who encourages you to continue pressing toward your vision?

5. How do you feel when people make negative comments about your vision?

Meditation Scriptures:

Habakkuk 2:2
Amos 3:7

Psalm 25:14
Romans 8:28
Proverbs 3:5-6

CHAPTER FOUR

Getting into Position

You make known to me the path of life, you will fill me with joy in your presence, with eternal pleasures at your right hand.

—Psalm 16:11NIV

LEAVING THE GOOD place is the first major hurdle we face when walking out our vision. It will require moving into unknown areas and learning new things. It means facing our fears and conquering them. It will require separating from certain people and places. It will require learning to walk until our faith catches up to us. But our destiny and our legacy are tied up in achieving the divine vision.

Fortunately, the overflow blessing is the proverbial pot of gold located at the end of the rainbow.

Joseph's vision could not come to pass in the land where he was born. It required him traveling to a foreign land where the people looked down on Hebrews as being inferior. It required him meeting with high-ranking officials and solving a problem that threatened a nation. Before this could happen, he would need to develop new skills and heal from past emotional scars before stepping into his destiny. All of this sounds nice, but there was one small problem with this scenario. Joseph was happy and content living in his homeland. Being the favorite child of his father meant he had no reason to leave his family voluntarily and travel to a foreign land. God orchestrated a series of events to get Joseph into the right place at the right time.

God sometimes allows things to happen in our lives in order to get us moving. As we move, He will give us directions on where to go. God is purposeful in where He wants us to go. Although the steps do not appear to be moving us toward our vision, they have a critical role in the process. There are several stops on the path He has leading to our destination. Each stop has a purpose in preparing us as believers to receive the overflow blessing.

The next time something happens to you, don't complain about the Devil attacking you. Instead, ask God if He is strategically positioning you. When God is positioning you, He is looking to accomplish the following things:

- *Reposition:* Move us outside of our comfort zone.

- *Preparation:* Grow and mature our character and skillsets.

- *Isolation:* Teach us to start depending on God.

- *Strategic Connections:* Enable us to reach our destination.

Okay, I hear your wheels turning. How can God accomplish these things if He doesn't come against our free will? Great question. Here is the answer. In order to accomplish these goals, God will allow circumstances to nudge us into taking action. As we start moving, He will illuminate the steps He wants us to take.

Staying on His ordained path requires us to be obedient to the leading of the Holy Spirit. This will require us to have daily communications with our Father in order for our spirit man to receive instruction. Our carnal man (or carnal nature) will want to reject the things of the Spirit. It desires to take us down different paths which seem good, but do not lead to our destiny. Each day we have to make a choice: am I following God's will for my life or am I doing my own thing? For those who choose to travel independent of God, that road often leads to a dead end, resulting in missed opportunities, frustration, and despair. For those who choose God's path, provision and blessings await. So, how does God guide His people?

Our modern GPS system reflects God's nature in many ways. This technology is designed to navigate a traveler from one place to another. All we have to do is enter our current location and our destination, and the system will generate several travel routes. Once we select the route and press start, it will issue driving instructions. One of the interesting things about this system is if we are on the right path, it will not say anything. If we have to travel twenty-eight miles on Interstate 42, it will not say anything as long as we are traveling on that road. When the system needs us to turn, it will warn us in advance. If we miss a turn, it will recalculate a new route to our destination and issue new instructions.

In many ways, this system mirrors how God directs His people. As we begin walking by faith, God will illuminate the steps for us to take. When we are on the right path, He may not say much. When it is time to make a change, He will issue new instructions. But this only applies to people who have left the familiar place. We will not experience this side of God if we are unwilling to walk into new territories by faith. That is the equivalent of turning on our car's GPS but being unwilling to back out of our driveway.

Let's explore why God needs to reposition us in order to receive the overflow blessing.

Reposition

The first step after the vision/revelation differs based on personality type. The adventurous type will immediately leap into action. The cautious type will want to see the route mapped out in a tangible form before they move. The steady type might refuse to move unless they are kicked out of their current spot. Don't worry, God has a way of nudging every personality type.

For Joseph, he needed to be kicked out of a predictable routine to start his journey toward his ultimate blessing. Let's face it, Joseph was not going to leave the familiarity of his family to travel to Egypt. He was adored by his father, and he held a special place of honor in the family. He knew the areas where the family's livestock grazed and could navigate the land independently. Despite having some angry brothers, there was no reason for him to leave home. But God's vision required just the opposite. But why did God allow Joseph to be sold into slavery?

The answer is simple. God placed the gift of management deep inside of Joseph. Like all of God's gifts, it was in seed form. It required activation and cultivation before it could be utilized effectively. For this to happen, Joseph needed a chance to manage something he was solely responsible for. Unfortunately, as the youngest child, he lacked opportunities to be in charge. His older brothers handled all the business for the family since Jacob was well into his years. After Joseph shared his dream with the family, I doubt if they ever allowed him to be in charge of anything.

Meanwhile, in a distant house in Egypt, Potiphar was busy with his official duties in addition to managing his large household. Although he was very successful, the demands on his time were tremendous. Imagine juggling a full-time job, a small business with employees, and a family. That does not leave a lot of time for a demanding wife. No wonder she had a wandering eye. He needed someone he could delegate some responsibility to. Neither man knew that one had the answer to the other's problem. But God had a divine plan to connect the two men and save a nation.

After Joseph revealed his second dream, his brothers contemplated his demise. On that fateful day, they grabbed him and threw him into a dry cistern. As they gathered to ponder his fate, Joseph pleaded with his brothers to get him out of the well. Several brothers proposed killing the self-centered young man. Thankfully, Judah was able to convince the brothers to spare Joseph's life. They sold him to some passing Ishmaelites traders, and his journey to Egypt began.

Since you are reading this book, I am confident that God is nudging you to start moving toward your destiny. No, this is not the Devil trying to steal your peace. No, people are not opposing you for no reason. God desires you to move into a new season which will require closing doors to the past. Unfortunately, many people struggle with this first step.

- Lord, I was just getting comfortable where I am.

- I have learned to master my job, and now I can enjoy success with minimal effort.

- You should be happy because I don't have to depend on You that much.

- I am self-sufficient and, truth be told, what can You do for me now?

So why does He want us to move? He needs us to move in order to prepare us to receive the blessing He has in store for us.

Character flaws and shallow thinking will cause the blessing to overwhelm us with detrimental effects. God uses seasons of trials and testing to grow and prepare the believer to walk out their destiny. Successfully completing this process is critical for receiving the overflow blessing.

Staying in the familiar place can be dangerous for the believer if God is calling us higher. Don't get me wrong, the familiar place is good for a season. But when it's time to move, staying longer will have negative repercussions. While the familiar place represents security and predictability, if we stay too long, it becomes a distraction that prevents us from walking down the path to our destiny. In some cases, staying in a position too long will cause us to block the blessing for the next person God wants to place in that role. It will cause us to miss time-sensitive open doors and connection.

When we become comfortable operating in our carnality, the spirit man suffers and so does our relationship with God. In the familiar place, we want to satisfy our flesh rather than obey God. Since the familiar place is very predictable, our faith does not grow, because we can do everything with our eyes closed. We can easily take our eyes off of God and allow our relationship with Him to atrophy.

We should never risk rebelling against God's will by staying too long in the familiar place.

Even Jesus had to leave the familiarity of His hometown in order to achieve His destiny. That was the place where everyone saw Him as the son of Joseph and Mary. Instead of seeing the Messiah who was in their midst, they only saw a carpenter's son. Due to the people's lack of faith, Jesus could perform few miracles in the city (Matthew 13:58). Because Jesus was familiar to them, the town's people could not see the power and authority He was walking in. He had to leave in order to fulfill His destiny. You, too, will have to leave the familiar place to achieve the destiny God has for you.

How do you know when it is time to leave the familiar place? Here is the first clue. When negative things start to happen in the place that was once a blessing, that is an indication of a season closing. This is not the Enemy attacking you. It is a signal that it is time to move. When God wanted Elijah to move from his resting place, He dried up the brook, which forced the prophet to go the widow's house in Zarephath (1 Kings 17:7-9).

I learned this lesson when I was playing on a church praise team. I had been playing keyboards faithfully for seven years, and it was an incredible blessing for me. In year eight, there was a leadership change, and things stopped being fun. The new leader wanted to take the praise team to a higher level, and I struggled to support the vision. In retrospect, I was still clinging to the vision of the old leader. The new wine didn't fit into my old wineskin.

Soon, negative comments started coming my way. I dreaded going to practice. I was torn between being loyal to the ministry and dealing with my feelings. When I finally made the decision to step down, weight was lifted from me, and I felt great peace. Unknown to me, there was a skilled musician who had just started attending the church who wanted to play on the praise team. When I stepped down, he stepped in and was able to embrace the leader's vision. This resulted in the worship team going to a new level. In parallel, God opened a new door for me to move into ministry. This taught me some powerful lessons about the familiar place:

- If you stay too long, the thing that brought you great joy will cause you great pain.
- You need to move when God commands you to move.
- You will block another person's blessing if you stay too long.
- There is something more for you to do.

Take us out of the familiar place and the storyline changes radically. It's amazing how well you can hear God's voice when you are traveling in an unfamiliar area. Our ears strain to hear the next set of instructions as we walk by faith. When we don't lean on our own understanding, we have to depend on the Lord to guide our footsteps as we traverse new territory. As a result, we pray more, we fast more, we read more, and we listen carefully for the next set of instructions. God is able to direct us as we walk in His divine purpose. When we have to depend on the Lord to navigate us through the unfamiliar place, our faith is strengthened as we trust Him more with our daily lives. We begin to confidently move when God says so because of his previous faithfulness. The story of Joseph illustrates the importance of leaving the familiar place.

For the nation of Israel, it was imperative that Joseph's brothers sold him into slavery. God needed to move Joseph out of Canaan and into Egypt where, one day, he would be in charge of everything in the land. Not only did God have to get Joseph to Egypt, but He allowed him to go through several trials in order to perfect his character and to make crucial connections. At the right time, God elevated His faithful servant and positioned him over all of Egypt.

When God moves you from a good place, He has a better place in mind for you. When He closes a door, He has a bigger door He wants to open for you. This will often require you to take a step backward before you can move forward. Joseph took a step backward when he lost his freedom and was sold into slavery. Then he leaped forward when God brought him before Pharaoh.

God wants to do the same thing for you, but know that the Enemy is watching you during this time. He will try to discourage you and ultimately get you to abandon the path God has you on by planting seeds of doubt such as:

- You know you had a good thing, but now it is gone.
- You have sinned, and God is punishing you now.
- You are not good enough to receive the promise of God.
- God doesn't care about you.
- God has forgotten about you.

This is the place where you have to resist the Enemy and proclaim Romans 8:28 over your life. *And we know that in all things God works for the good of those who love him, who have been called according to his purpose* (NIV). God has a plan for your life. He will never leave or forsake you (Hebrews 13:5). Continually speak God's promises as you seek out the new door He has for you.

Sometimes God allows things to happen because others are depending on us to achieve our purpose. In his rebellion against God, Jonah boarded a ship that was headed in the opposite direction of Nineveh. He did not want to go and deliver the harsh word from God. But God had a plan, so He allowed a terrible storm to engulf the ship. In a panic, the crew tossed Jonah into the sea. Then a whale swallowed him and deposited him at Nineveh three days later (Jonah 1 and 2).

Please note that while certain aspects of the plan looked scary, nothing harmed Jonah. He made it safely to Nineveh, where he delivered a stern warning to the people. But their response shocked Jonah. Instead of continuing in their evil ways, they were convicted by the prophetic warning. They repented and saved the city. Jonah's disobedience almost resulted in the destruction of an entire city. But God had a plan.

If He has allowed a door to close on you, then rest assured He has something bigger in store for you.

Preparation

God cannot give us the overflow blessing when He gives us the revelation of our future. Why? Because we are not ready for it. We do not have the capacity to embrace all that the blessing has with it.

My pastor taught this concept using the story of a person who sacrificed to buy a high-performance luxury car. At first, they were very happy with their purchase. But then came the higher costs associated with insurance, maintenance, and fuel consumption. The blessing which initially brought so much joy, drained their bank account. The cost of a simple oil change was now $150 (vs. $45 at Jiffy Lube) and the cost of a new battery plus installation $1000 (instead of $150 at Advance Auto or Auto Zone). This person failed to fully understand the hidden expense of owning a high-performance vehicle. They suffered financial hardship, because they did not plan for the incremental operating cost associated with that vehicle model. If they would have moved in God's timing, they would have had sufficient income to absorb the complete cost of ownership.

Unfortunately, many want the blessing without going through the season of preparation. Let's be honest for a second. Are you really ready to receive?

Proverbs 10:22 says, *The blessing of the Lord, it maketh rich, and He addeth no sorrow with it* (KJV). Why? Because He will not give us our blessing before we are ready. He knows our character, experience level, and maturity are insufficient to receive all that He has for us. Like a good father, He doesn't want our character flaws to penalize us at this new level. He doesn't want our lack of patience dealing with people to disqualify us. He doesn't want our emotional immaturity to get us kicked out of the blessed place. To prepare us to receive, He will allow us to go through a process.

The first step is getting us into the right position. God could not give Joseph the high-ranking position in Pharaoh's kingdom without preparing him. Let's face it, Joseph had a lot to learn when he arrived at Potiphar's house. Plus, he needed opportunities to develop the management seed God had placed inside of him.

Going back to the story, Joseph was eventually purchased by Potiphar and brought to his house. In this new environment, the management seed had an opportunity to sprout. Joseph quickly excelled at everything he was tasked to do. Finally, he had a chance to exercise the gift of management. People quickly realized the favor of the Lord rested on Joseph, and he was soon given responsibility for the entire house. With Joseph in charge, the only thing Potiphar worried about was what he wanted to eat each day. In retrospect, Joseph's arrival was a wonderful blessing for Potiphar.

During this time, Joseph learned how to make sound decisions. He learned how to work with people and delegate responsibilities. He learned how to hold people accountable and make things happen through others. He had opportunities to improve his communication skills and establish his integrity.

With the successful completion of each task, Joseph was given more responsibility. Being cast into slavery positioned Joseph for the opportunity to develop the gifts God placed inside of him. One might argue that Joseph could have had similar opportunities at home, but with that many older brothers, it is highly doubtful he would have had an opportunity to grow his management skills.

God will use negative things to position us in opportunities to develop our gifts and talents. The doors that closed for you were designed to get you moving toward a new and bigger opportunity. If you are in the preparation process, don't stop. Keep pressing forward. If you are just leaving the comfortable place, get ready for an incredible journey.

Isolation

After leaving the familiar place, God will allow us to experience a season of isolation, which is designed to bring focus on God. During this time, He will allow friendships to wane and relationships to fail. No matter how hard we try to connect with people, we continually find ourselves alone and isolated. This is not the work of the Devil. He does not have that kind of power in our lives. This is not punishment for our sins, although the quiet time gives us opportunities to reflect on the seeds we have sown.

We ask, *Lord, what are you doing?*

God uses this quiet time to teach us to hear his voice. He desires that we commune with Him on a daily basis, not just on Sunday. He wants us to seek His input daily on our actions, needs, and concerns. When we make time to be still in His presence, He speaks to us and answers our prayers. When we do this on a consistent basis, we develop a relationship with God and learn to trust Him. No longer lobbing prayers across the wall and waiting to see the manifestation, we commune with him frequently during the course of our day.

Now let's be real, God is not going to compete for our attention. He will not go against our free will. If we want to ask for advice from Jason or Jacqueline instead of God, we are free to do so. But when their advice has us circling the block again to face the same test and trials, maybe we will seek guidance from a different source the next time around.

Isolation gives us time for introspection. It causes us to look at our decisions, our character, and our guidance source. During this time, God will reveal things about the condition and content of our heart. This can be quite painful when we realize we are not as great as we perceive ourselves. But that is one of Gods intended outcomes for this time.

Warning: This is not the time to harden your heart and dismiss what God reveals about you.

Failure to address these issues will result in us wandering around the desert until we pass this step. Fortunately, God is faithful and will not abandon us while we are taking the test repeatedly. But rest assured, we will face the same test again and again until we pass. Each failure results in additional delays on the journey to our destiny. When this happens, we want to complain and blame God. But the harsh reality is the delay is the consequence of our actions. *Ouch, that hurts!*

David had to wait fifteen years from the time he was anointed by Samuel until he assumed his leadership position. For much of that time, David was in isolation, hiding from King Saul. He had been removed from the position of leading the army and was no longer welcomed in Saul's inner circle. Once a valued servant, David found himself running from Saul, who desired to kill him. In *Facing Your Giants,* Max Lucado states that David found refuge in God while he was hiding from Saul. The word *refuge* means a condition of being safe or sheltered from pursuit, danger, or trouble. When he had no other options, David turned his face to God.

During this time, David wrote most of the book of Psalms. I love this book, because it gives readers great insight into the nature and heart of God. It also serves as an example of the type of relationship we can have with God. God was David's friend and confidant. In Psalm 57, David described his plight and how God spared him from his enemies. The Scriptures tell of how David survived by taking shelter in the shadow of God's wings until the disaster passed.

When we find ourselves isolated for a season, we need to turn our focus solely toward God. Max Lucado summed this up eloquently when he wrote, "You will never know that Jesus is all you need until He is all that you have." Because when the Lord is all we have, we discover He is all we need. Not our family, not our friends, and not our jobs. Yes, there is a blessing in the isolation.

Another benefit from isolation is that we are removed from the thoughts and opinions of carnal people. Those who would have us question our divine vision. Those who would tell us to stop pursuing this dream and stay in the familiar place. They can't see their own vision, so they certainly can't see ours. The Enemy knows that if we are around too much negativity concerning our vision, it will erode our faith and cause us to doubt God.

Imagine how negative Joseph's brothers felt concerning his dream:

- Who does he think he is?

- Why would we bow down to him?

- Our father may like you, but we don't have to like you.

- Get out of here with your crazy dreams.

- That is never going to happen.

God had a plan, and He had to remove Joseph from everyone who could not embrace his destiny. He could not allow the family's simple view of their lives to thwart the plan He had for saving a nation. When an eagle understands his destiny is in the sky, he will cease clinging to ground. The negative action of being enslaved had a positive outcome, because Joseph was removed from family naysayers.

Isolation serves to protects us from negative and fearful people who desire to poison our vision. When the isolation comes, we should embrace it and concentrate on hearing His voice. The isolation is designed to protect and hide us while we are in the preparation process.

Here are some interesting quotes I found to be encouraging on this matter:

- *Keep away from people who try to belittle your ambitions. Small people always do that, but the really great make you feel that you, too, can become great.* ~ Mark Twain

- *People seldom improve when they have no other model but themselves to copy.* ~ Oliver Goldsmith

- *Never listen to human plans. God can work mightily when you persist in believing Him in spite of discouragement from the human standpoint... I am moved by what I believe. I know this: No man looks at the circumstances if he believes.* ~ Smith Wigglesworth

While researching this subject, I found a wonderful story to illustrate the value of being isolated for a season. Thomas Alva Edison was a great American inventor and businessman. Yet as a child, he struggled in the classroom. His persistent questions and self-centered behavior could be characterized under the modern-day diagnoses of ADHD (Attention Deficit Hyperactivity Disorder). This resulted in the teacher expelling young Thomas after only twelve weeks of school.

In a letter to his mother, the teacher said that Thomas had a learning disability and would never amount to anything. But my guess is the teacher had never experienced a child as brilliant as Thomas. His mother commenced to teaching him the "Three Rs" (reading, writing, and arithmetic) and the Bible at home. In this isolation, away from negative people and their shallow thoughts, the highly intelligent child was able to excel in all his subjects. Without the limitations of the familiar place, he cultivated the gifts inside of him. He went on to be a highly successful business man (founder of General Electric Company) and was credited with over 1000 patents. His most notable inventions include the lightbulb, the phonograph, and the motion picture camera.

God had a plan for Thomas Edison, and He has a wonderful plan for you.

Strategic Connection

God is faithful to provide provision for divine visions. He has placed people and resources on the path to our destiny that He is illuminating. Obedience is critical for accessing all He has prepared for us. Think about this:

- There are people who have unique problems only you can solve.

- There are people looking to invest in your idea.

- There are people who are capable of bringing your vision to life.

- There are people who want to hire you for your unique skills and abilities.

- There are people who want to elevate you because you have the leadership skills to complete their vision.

The challenge is in finding these people. Fear not, God will direct your steps so that you meet these people at the appointed time. Whatever you need to achieve the vision, God will provide for you. The secret is you have to allow Him to lead you to the provision. Sometimes, the path He takes you down will require sacrificing your flesh for a season. Joseph had to crucify his flesh when he was sold into slavery. But God was setting him up to meet people who had a role in bringing his vision to pass.

It was crucial that Potiphar purchased Joseph to serve in his house. Potiphar was one of Pharaoh's officials and the captain of the guard. He had direct access to Pharaoh and his top leaders. After serving Potiphar for several years, Joseph caught the wandering eye of his wife. When he refused her advances, she accused Joseph of trying to assault her. Subsequently, Joseph was thrown into the king's jail. This was no ordinary jail. This was the place where Pharaoh sent his officials to be held for punishment.

While serving his sentence, Joseph met the chief cup bearer and the chief baker. In a short period of time, Joseph went from being hundreds of miles from Pharaoh to now being one person away. Because he had been thrown into the king's jail, he was in position to interpret the dreams of the king's officials.

Fast forward two years. Pharaoh was bothered by a series of dreams about cows. He sent for all the wise men and magicians in the land, but no one could interpret the dream. Then the chief cup bearer remembered the man who interpreted his own dream while he was in prison and recommended him to Pharaoh. Joseph was in the right place to interpret the dreams of the king and solve a problem for the nation.

Being in the right place at the right time is critical for receiving what God has for us. That is why we cannot stay in the familiar place too long. We will miss out on divine connections, crucial training, and preparatory experiences. But some choose to stay in the comfort of the familiar place. They don't want to change, and they forfeit many things God wants to do in their lives.

When we know how to do everything in the comfortable place, there is no need for faith. Sure, we can believe God exists, but we don't give Him a chance to reveal more of His glory. Instead of operating in faith, we choose to operate in our carnal knowledge where we can manage everything ourselves. But it is impossible to obtain the overflow blessing without God.

It's time to get moving. There are people to meet who will have an impact on your destiny. When you feel the gentle nudging of the Holy Spirit to go to an event, go. When the Holy Spirit tells you to talk to a person, be obedient. Sometimes it's a sign of a potential divine connection. Divine connections can be in the form of people, but they can also be in the form of opportunities or new information. They will always link back to the original vision, although it may take some time to realize it. When we listen to His voice, He will lead us to fulfill the vision He deposited in us. So, why are you still standing there?

Chrystal loved music and always wanted to be in entertainment. After receiving her law degree from the University of North Carolina (UNC), she worked in private practice for several years before being appointed to serve as a judge on the North Carolina Industrial Commission in 1995. In this position, she presided over worker's compensation proceedings. But she still desired to be involved in music.

This was a politically appointed position, and it came with some restrictions concerning outside businesses. In 2008, we were asked to write music for a church play, so we formed Mad Praise, a music publishing company. Chrystal's involvement was severely limited due to potential conflicts of interest with her political job. But God was working.

In 2012, the state elected a republican governor who brought sweeping changes to the state. In 2013, he sought to replace all the appointed incumbents at the Industrial Commission with his choices. Chrystal was forced to leave her job. Fortunately, she was allowed to retire after twenty years of service.

But God had a plan for her. He opened the door for her to step into practicing family law, and she hit the ground with a flood of business. In parallel, the contacts we had cultivated in the music industry sought her expertise on entertainment law. Slowly, her private practice steadily shifted to a mix of family law and entertainment law. Looking back over her life, we can see how God used each situation to move her closer to the vision He had placed in her. He is always faithful.

Where is God calling you to go? Are you clinging to your past, or have you jumped into the new territory? One thing is certain: if you don't move, you will forfeit your blessing.

Summary

Chasing our destiny requires leaving the comfortable place and traveling in unfamiliar areas. When God allows a door to be closed, we must accept the fact and be willing to move into the new season. Fortunately, the new season represents opportunities for personal growth and character development. It provides us with opportunities to be strategically positioned and develop new relationships. During this season, our preparation translates into increasing the size of our tent to receive the overflow blessing. The extent to which we can stretch our tent (develop our capacity) determines the amount of the blessing we can contain.

The Bible is full of examples of people who had to leave the familiar place to achieve God's plan for their lives. The Lord ordered Abram to leave Haran, the land of his father, and travel to a distant land. He promised Abram He would make him into a great nation and that his name would be great (Genesis 12:1-2). Abram had to leave the familiar place in order to put things in motion that would fulfill the promises of God.

The Lord directed Joshua to leave the desert where the Israelites had been wandering for forty years, cross the Jordan River, and claim the land God had promised for them (Joshua 1:1-10). He gave them favor in conquering and settling the land.

The prophet Samuel had to leave his family to serve in the house of the high priest Eli and be mentored by him. He went on to be a powerful leader for Israel as well as anointing their first two kings.

What door are you trying to keep open? Are you hanging on to relationships whose time has passed? Why are you interacting with old friends who are determined to stay in their familiar place? Or those family members who can't see where God is taking you. Those who scoff at your dreams and speak to the way things have always been done. Don't allow their fears to prevent you from chasing your destiny. Instead of despairing about lost jobs, friends, and family, focus on the new things God wants to do in your life. I remember my grandmother saying when one door closes, another door opens. This phrase captures a key aspect of the process God uses to prepare us for our blessing.

Don't be alarmed when a season comes to an end. Don't try and hold on to the past and risk missing the future. Understand that God will not put the new opportunity in your hand until you empty your hand. Conventional wisdom says "a bird in the hand is worth two in the bush." But following this thinking eliminates the need for faith. It takes faith to let go of an opportunity before God provides a new one. And the Bible says *without faith, it is impossible to please God* (Hebrews 11:6 NIV).

Often, the hardest part of walking toward the vision is leaving familiar things behind. Joseph had to leave his family in order to walk in his purpose. We will have to do the same in order to achieve God's plan for our lives.

So, dust your feet off, and keep moving toward your vision. There is an overflow blessing waiting for you when you arrive. *The journey of a thousand miles begins with a single step* (Lao Tzu).

Reflection Points:

1. What door has God closed for you?

2. What does He want you to learn from your current situation?

3. Is God prompting you to move outside your comfortable place and experience something new?

4. What steps are you taking to hear His voice?

5. What divine connections have you made in the past year?

6. Who has God separated you from?

Meditation Scriptures

2 Timothy 1:7
Isaiah 41:13
Psalm 27:14
Psalm 25:4
Psalm 27:11
Romans 15:13

CHAPTER FIVE

The Preparation Process

God doesn't call the equipped, He equips the called.
—Rick Yancey

HOW MANY OF you experienced playing sports in high school? Were you one of those people who enjoyed playing the game but hated practice?

In the weeks leading up to the start of football practice, I talked with my high school friends about what type of season we were going to have. But before we could play a game, we had to go through several weeks of grueling practices. The coaches used a multitude of drills to improve our physical condition and refine the basic skills for each position. Then they had us run numerous exercises to learn how to operate as a team. Finally, we had several scrimmages to put all the pieces together and make adjustments. Once we completed our preparation, we played our first game.

While most of us loved to play the game, the majority disliked the preparation process. Looking back, I realize our preparation and commitment to those practices had a significant impact on how well we played during the season. The year we had our toughest practices was the year we had our best record. That experience taught me preparation is the key to being successful in anything we do in life. The same principle applies to kingdom citizens who are following God's plan for their lives. Preparation always precedes the divine elevation.

My grandmother, Vivien King Bright, used to say it was better to go in the little end of the horn and out the big end rather than vice versa. While this didn't make sense to me when I was young, when I entered college, I realized it was better to have learning opportunities early on in life to prepare me rather than later when they could be a real problem.

Look at the statistics with lottery winners. Data indicates that 70 percent of lottery winners are broke within seven years. Researchers determined that poor money management skills result in people squandering away their fortunes. To put it bluntly, they were not prepared to handle that level of blessing. Clearly, it is no fun getting a big blessing and then going through the extremely painful process of learning how to manage it. Thankfully, God will not release the blessing before we are capable of receiving it.

Prepare to Succeed

Whatever God has called us to do, He has a plan to prepare us to achieve our destiny. His plan calls for the believer to go through a season of trials and testing to equip us and mature our faith. During this time, God will allow circumstances to happen that will grow us in our understanding of His will, His ways, and His Word. When we exit the process, we are able to shine brightly, because we have been transformed into His image.

The Bible says we are to count it all joy when we are tested, because we know the trying of our faith develops patience (James 1:2). We must allow patience to complete her perfect work that we may be whole and complete, lacking nothing. God wants us to be prepared to receive. He realizes the magnitude of His wonderful blessing would totally overwhelm us in our current state. He nudges us to embark on a journey to equip us so the blessing brings prosperity and not sorrow.

The preparation process can be a very challenging time for the believer. Let's face it, God's timing doesn't always align with our own sense of time. Consequently, this season can span several years. This is where the Enemy starts whispering, *Didn't God promise you this?* Doubt creeps into our daily thinking. If left unchecked, it will erode our faith and weaken our resolve. Soon, we begin to question if we really heard from God. Then comes the ultimatum: *God if that was You, give me a sign.* Some will reach the end of their rope and scream *I quit!* They abort the God-sanctioned preparation process due to frustration, despair, and hopelessness. This is sad, because God had a magnificent blessing in store for them. But for those who can endure and complete the process, there will be a season of bountiful harvest when the reaper shall pass the sower (Amos 9:13). God will redeem all that was lost or stolen during the season of preparation. The trials and tests are truly for our good.

Below are four things God wants to accomplish during the season of preparation:

- Strengthen our faith.
- Develop our skills and abilities.
- Refine our character.
- Mature the believer.

In the previous chapter, we learned God will allow things to happen to move us out of the familiar place. He will allow us to go through seasons of challenges and tests to prepare us. During this time, we can expect the Enemy to attack us by planting seeds of doubt and anxiety. His goal is to discourage us so we will abort the process and forfeit our destiny. This season might start out with what appears to be a bad thing happening to us. Joseph's rise to power started with him being sold into slavery.

Why Did this Happen?

Like many Christians, I used to wonder why bad things happen to God's people. Especially since the Bible says He has plans to prosper us and give us a hope and a future (Jeremiah 29:11). Here are some of the questions I have asked over the course of my Christian walk. Do they sound familiar?

- Why did my marriage fail?
- Why did this church hurt occur?
- Why was I released from my job?
- Why didn't I get the job?
- Why have I been forced to take this new assignment?
- God, this is not what I wanted for my life. This can't be You, God. This must be the work of the Enemy. Is he trying to hold me down and block my blessing?

Experience has taught me that many times what I thought was bad, was actually for my good. It was not the Enemy trying to hinder me. The bad things gave way to opportunities to do and experience new things, to develop new skills, and to navigate in new areas. In fact, everything that happens to a believer is for a specific purpose. Romans 8:28 states that *in all things, God works for the good of those who love who love Him, who have been called according to His purpose* (NIV). Nothing is wasted. Every experience, whether good or bad, translates into a learning or ministry opportunity for the believer.

Let's address one misconception I have heard believers state many times. We are quick to blame the Enemy for negative things that happen in our lives. We love to respond by engaging him in spiritual warfare. But let me share this secret: the Enemy does not have authority over our lives. The story of Job shows us that Satan can only do what God allows him to do, and he must answer to God concerning his actions. Yet somehow, believers have embraced erroneous teachings that attribute more power to the Enemy than what he really has. If we believe God is sovereign, then the Enemy can do nothing without His permission.

Satan could only afflict Job after God took down the hedge of protection surrounding him. God allowed that to happen for a reason. But rest assured, in our lives He is working everything out for our good. Stop fighting the Enemy and start pressing toward your destiny.

I acknowledge that some bad things are the direct consequence of our actions and sin. But the rest is part of God's plan to prepare and strengthen us. So, let's stop fighting God and focus on getting through the process, because these trials provide us with opportunities to grow and mature as Christians. We need dysfunctional emotional wounds exposed and healed. Unhealthy thoughts and actions need to be uncovered and purged. Selfish motives must be brought out of the darkness into the marvelous light of Christ Jesus. Our soul (our will, intellect, desires, dreams) must be transformed, and our countenance should reflect the love of Christ. How will they know we are Christians? When they see the fruit of the spirit in our daily behaviors. Who is ready for new growth?

Once we have demonstrated a level of maturity that will allow us to handle the blessing, then God fulfills His promise. He will release a blessing we will not have room enough to contain. Proverbs 10:22 says, *the blessing of the Lord makes one rich, and He adds no sorrow with it* (NKJV). The Bible also states in Psalm 84:11, *For the Lord God is a sun and shield; the Lord will give grace and glory; no good thing will he withhold from them that walk uprightly* (KVJ). God will allow a season of preparation to train believers to walk righteously. Let's examine each of the points God wants to achieve during the preparation process.

Strengthening Our Faith

People who engage in weight training go to the gym several times a week to develop their muscles. They engage in rigorous exercises that cause their muscles to stretch and grow. They eat special diets and often take supplements to facilitate muscle development. Over time, faithful adherence to this regimen will deliver the desired muscular physique.

Similarly, our faith needs to be exercised in order for it to grow and develop. Life trials and challenges provide the resistance that causes our faith to grow. As we exercise our faith during a trial, God reveals more of His glory, and our faith increases. We must continually operate in faith in order to please God. Hebrews 11:6 says that *without faith, it is impossible to please God, because anyone who comes to Him must believe that He exists and that He rewards those who earnestly seek Him* (NIV).

First, let's define faith. The dictionary defines it as the complete trust or confidence in someone or something. Hebrews 11:1 refers to faith as the assurance of things hoped for and the evidence of things not seen. Stated differently, it is trusting in something you can not explicitly prove. When we operate in faith, it often means doing things before we fully understand the *why*. It means doing things when we cannot see the end result. For many, it means doing things we never thought we could do.

Let's discuss the paradox of the familiar place. When we do not vary our daily routines, they become familiar. We gain confidence and a sense of security from the predictable nature of the routines. The lack of variance soothes our anxiety, and we tend to worry less. Life is enjoyable, because it is predictable and controllable.

On the other hand, it is amazing how much we pray and seek God's face when trials or testing move us out of the familiar place. Our sense of security shatters when things don't go as we planned. Over time, anxiety and fear will creep in due to the level of uncertainty in our lives. We seriously seek God's face to guide us through these difficult times. Surviving in this place requires faith in order to navigate across the unfamiliar territory.

When Joseph was sold into slavery, he was separated from everything he knew. He traveled into new territory and would soon be dealing with people who looked down on Hebrews with disdain. No longer would he be involved in managing livestock for his family. No longer would he be the favored son with all the corresponding privileges. God moved Joseph way outside his comfort zone. He could not rely on past experiences to guide him, because everything was different from what he was used to. He had never been enslaved, he had never worked in a house, and he had never led a nation. How did Joseph prosper in each situation? By relying solely on his relationship with God to guide him.

Like young David tending his sheep on a hillside, Joseph cultivated this relationship while he traveled back and forth between his father's tent and the flocks in the fields. It was his relationship that allowed him to survive the trip to Egypt in bondage. Joseph learned to face each new situation by faith, knowing God would see him through. He knew that by faith:

- God would show him how to deal with emotional pain, lead people, and manage resources.

- He would turn a negative situation into a positive one while serving in Potiphar's house.

- He could endure being thrown in jail due to the false accusations of Potiphar's wife.

- He was able to interpret the dreams of Pharaoh's officials.

- He endured the jail for two more years after the chief butler forgot about him.

- He could interpret Pharaoh's dreams.

Is your faith strong enough to get you through the season you are in?

For Joseph, each setback provided him with an opportunity to develop the gift of management buried deep inside. All he needed was an opportunity that would allow the seed to blossom, grow, and produce fruit. Initially, Joseph was not qualified to manage a large household with servants and slaves. Nor was he qualified to run a jail. But his faith in God enabled him to be successful in both situations. These challenges prepared him to one day manage the richest nation of that age. All because he moved by faith in each challenging season.

If you are willing to move by faith, God will do the same thing for you.

The Bible is filled with great men and women of faith. Those who, despite their personal flaws, were ultimately used by God to do great things. By faith:

- Abram traveled to Mount Moriah to sacrifice his son. He heard God's voice and was obedient.

- Ruth obeyed the instructions of Naomi while gleaning in the fields of Boaz.

- David met Goliath armed only with a sling shot and some rocks.

- The woman with the issue of blood pressed through the crowd of people to touch the garment of Jesus.

- Moses led the Israelites out of Egypt.

- Joseph served faithfully in the house of Potiphar where he learned how to manage effectively.

God used the challenging times to prepare each of them for a larger blessing.

Here is a slightly different explanation of faith that I believe is relevant today. *Faith sees the invisible, believes the incredible, and receives the impossible* (Corrie Ten Boom).

How do we exercise our faith? By being obedient to His commandments and His will for our lives. When we hear His voice, we must obey and do what He says. We must be willing to sacrifice our desires and wants in order to do what God wants. In his first letter to the church in Corinth, Paul wrote that our faith *should not stand in the wisdom of men but in the power of God* (I Corinthians 2:5 KJV). The carnal man does not understand the things of God. Only the spirit man can comprehend what God is doing. Believers have learned not to lean on their understanding because eyes haven't seen, ears haven't heard, and hearts have not understood the things God has prepared for those who love him (vs. 9). When we put His Word to the test and it comes back true, we trust God more.

As our faith increases, we slowly release more control of our lives to God. The challenge for modern-day believers is not to get distracted by the test or the setback. Instead of complaining, we should look at every situation as a learning opportunity. When I am facing challenging times, I have learned to ask God, *what do You want me to learn from this situation?* For me, exercising my faith means learning to walk and letting my faith catch up.

In retrospect, losing my job in 2012 was a tremendous blessing. It allowed me time to take care of my mother during the last sixteen months of her life. It was during this time that God gave me a vision for my music. As I drew closer to Him, I had opportunities to minister God's Word to others, which eventually opened the door for me in ministry. Rather than lamenting about why this bad thing happened, I asked God daily what He wanted me to do. I learned to depend on Him for my daily provision as well as ordering my footsteps. With each act of obedience, God revealed more of His glory, which enabled my faith to grow.

During this season, when people said I was wasting time, I grew spiritually and experienced many signs and wonders. I was able to play for different ministry events that allowed me to witness miraculous healings, manifestations of gold flakes and gem stones, and angelic beings. I was able to learn about my spiritual gifts and attend training on how to use them. As a musician, I learned to play prophetically and to flow in the Spirit.

I remember playing for some events where I just looked at my hands playing things I had never practiced or played before. The Holy Spirit took over and used me to release a new sound along with my worship colleagues. I experienced prophecies over my life that came true, and I came to understand that the spiritual realm is just as real as the natural realm.

Most importantly, I learned to see with both my natural and my spiritual eyes. This enabled me to deal with situations more effectively while maintaining my peace and joy. My faith grew exponentially during this time of setback. Looking back, I realize God was strengthening my faith for the journey ahead.

Don't get me wrong, I struggled with losing my job. My flesh wanted to get another job. But God gave me a confirming word through Joel Osteen. I was channel surfing when I paused on his television show. He was teaching and said, "*That* had to happen, so that *this* could happen." Those words and his subsequent message ministered to me and reminded me that God had a plan for me.

He also has a plan for you, a plan to prosper you. I encourage you to rejoice and proclaim that God is in control. He is bigger than your problems, and He will never leave you or forsake you. Stop worrying. Allow that challenge to be a learning opportunity. It may seem insignificant now, but it has a part to play in where you are going.

What are you doing by faith? Has your faith grown from the trials you have faced?

Developing Our Skills and Abilities.

The season of preparation gives us an opportunity to develop and improve our natural abilities. It is a time where we develop confidence in our talents and our God. When we look at the story of Joseph, it is hard to see what he was good at other than sharing negative reports about his brothers. But when we look at what happened after he was sold into slavery, we see the emergence of a natural leader with strong management skills.

When the Ishmaelite traders reached Egypt, they sold Joseph to an Egyptian named Potiphar. Potiphar was a person of significance in his day. He was an officer of Pharaoh, and he served as the captain of the guard. His position afforded him the luxury of having a house managed by servants and slaves. It was here that Joseph distinguished himself from other slaves. In his first opportunity to operate independent of his brothers, Joseph made the best of a negative situation. He excelled at every task assigned to him and was eventually given greater levels of responsibilities by his master.

God's favor shined upon Joseph, and he became very successful. Potiphar recognized the Lord was with Joseph and made all that he touched prosper. How did Potiphar recognize the hand of the Lord on Joseph? Was it because of the joy Joseph had while serving his master? Was it because of the exceptional quality of his work? Was it because of his positive attitude? While we may never know the exact answer, it is clear Joseph was both a hard worker and a person of integrity. He was able to foster teamwork and unify the hearts of others to achieve the master's wishes.

Eventually, Potiphar made Joseph the overseer of his house. In this role, Joseph was responsible for managing all aspects of the house: the resources, the processes, and the business interactions. The Bible says the Lord blessed the Egyptian's house for Joseph's sake, and the blessing of the Lord was upon both the house and the field. This is where Joseph's management skills were tested and developed. Despite not having previous leadership experience, Joseph was obedient to the leading of the Lord, and everything he touched prospered.

It is clear that Joseph took advantage of his time in bondage to develop new skills. How are you viewing the challenges you are facing this week? Are you complaining about how things are unfair? Are you whining and walking around with a negative attitude? Or are you viewing it as an opportunity for improvement and growth? Your success will be determined by how you respond to the challenges of life. Often, the toughest situations are really a blessing in disguise. They provide us with wonderful opportunities to develop and perfect our skills. When we successfully overcome these challenges, we are viewed as being ready for higher levels of responsibility. The secret is to have the right attitude when you have challenges.

Years ago, motivational speaker Zig Ziglar declared, "It's your attitude, more than your aptitude, that will determine your altitude." It is imperative to view each challenge and trial as an opportunity to improve. If you sense that you are in a season of preparation, what new things have you been exposed to?

Developing Our Character

When gold is mined from the earth, it must go through a refining process to remove impurities. In biblical times, the metal was placed in a crucible and heated to 1,943 degrees Fahrenheit in a furnace. Once the metal reached the liquid phase, the craftsman would slowly stir the molten metal and skim off the impurities that rose to the top. This process was repeated several times until there were no impurities to be removed. The resultant metal was considered pure. God uses a similar process to shape and refine our character using fiery trials and challenges.

What happens when we have character issues? Will they disqualify us from the blessing God wants to supply us with? According to Abram (liar) and Jacob (deceiver) and David (adulterer), the answer is no. They all went through seasons of trials to refine their character in order to walk out their divine purpose. Many times, God allows trials to uncover character flaws that must be addressed before the believer can be elevated. Flaws that will cause great harm if they are carried into the next level God has for us. The following story illustrates this point.

Jerry was excited to be interviewing for an executive position with a large company. This had been his professional goal for many years. He had done exceptionally well with the morning interviews, and now he was scheduled to have lunch with the company CEO. As they walked through the company cafeteria, Jerry casually picked up two packs of butter and put them in his pocket. The CEO took notice, especially when the cashier did not charge him for them.

My mother always told me that taking something and not paying for it was stealing. Why would Jerry do such a thing, especially on this important day? Maybe this was a subconscious habit he had been doing for years. For the CEO, this simple act was a glaring red flag concerning Jerry's integrity. If he was willing to steal butter, what would he do overseeing multi-million-dollar business transactions. Rather than put the company at risk, the CEO decided to continue interviewing other candidates. Despite his previous success, Jerry did not receive an offer because of the flaw in his character.

How many of us have been disqualified from opportunities because of flaws in our character? For some, the flaw is our temper. For some, it is our critical spirit. And for others, it is our nasty mouth or lust of the eyes. If this is resonating with you, maybe the challenges you are facing are meant to purge you from things that will block your future.

For Joseph, it was his pride. While his brothers labored in the fields tending to the flocks, Joseph served as the messenger boy for his father. He went back and forth snitching on his brothers to their father. This behavior spawned anger in his brothers. When Jacob gave Joseph a special coat signifying favor, this further alienated his brothers. The final straw came when he shared his dream with his brothers. This caused them to burn with indignation at the thought of bowing down to their younger brother. When he shared his second dream with them, they became even more incensed. This upset his parents, and Jacob rebuked Joseph and quickly dismissed the matter. Who was this arrogant young man proclaiming that his mother and father would bow down to him? But God was going to use this flaw to move Joseph into his divine destiny. *Pride goes before destruction, a haughty spirit before a fall* (Proverbs 16:18 NIV).

It was after Joseph revealed his second dream that his brothers plotted to get rid of him. Joseph's world changed drastically. He went from a position of prominence in his father's household to irrelevance as he walked across the desert sands chained to other slaves. No longer could he have his way. He had been stripped of his prominent coat, his exalted place in his family, and his freedom. All control over his life had been taken away, and now he was forced to serve others.

The next thirteen years in bondage broke the spirit of pride that existed when he was living with his family. Although he was able to have success and gain prominence in Potiphar's house, he again found himself in obscurity when he was thrown into the jail. But the pressure of faithfully serving in both situations starved his pride and fostered a spirit of humility. The time in bondage resulted in the death of the selfish young man and the emergence of God's humble servant. Joseph realized he was serving and honoring his God by serving his human, earthly masters in excellence. How many of us honor God with our behavior on our jobs?

But Joseph had a second character flaw that needed to be addressed. He was angry with his brothers for the horrible crime they had committed. It grieved him and vexed his spirit as he traveled in the caravan to Egypt. But unlike many of us, Joseph did not allow these negative emotions to define his life. Rather than having a pity party, he focused on being the best person he could be, given the circumstances. Yes, he had been wronged. Yes, he had a right to be angry and bitter. But that did not cause him to give up and quit. Instead, he put all his energy into the task at hand. And the Bible makes it clear he was very successful working for Potiphar.

How many of us could have responded to a negative situation like Joseph? The wisdom of the modern world would have us consumed by anger and bitterness. Forget trying to do well in our current situation, we would be too busy lamenting about the wrong doing. We would complain excessively to our friends, coworkers, and bosses. Some would go so far as to post it all over social media. But how many would reflect on the situation as a learning opportunity from God?

In the season of preparation, it is important to make the best of every situation. I remember my grandmother saying when life gives you lemons, you have to make lemonade. Her mother shared that with her as they managed to live in the segregated South governed by hateful Jim Crow laws. They struggled to rise above their circumstances to both get college degrees, marry college-educated men, and to acquire several pieces of property. Instead of reacting to the negative challenges of those times, they chose to be the best they could be. They turned those painful life lessons into a solid foundation of values and a work ethic that enabled them to overachieve. I am grateful those lessons have been passed down through the generations of my family.

Character flaws will cause believers to rebel against God's commandments, resulting in grave consequences. When the Israelites attacked the city of Ai, they were soundly defeated. This defeat came as a shock to the Israelites after the miraculous victory at Jericho. A perplexed Joshua inquired of the Lord and was told there was sin in the camp. This sin had to be purged before God would support the Israelites in conquering the promised land. Joshua went through the entire camp until the origin of the sin was identified and addressed. The problem was traced to Aichen, who confessed to coveting some of the treasure. This character flaw caused him to commit a sin which ultimately cost him his life. Once the sin was eradicated, the favor of the Lord returned, and the Israelites resumed marching victoriously into the promised land.

Character flaws that lead us to sin will cause us to veer off of the path God has for us. Once we leave the path, we must confront issues in our own strength. In some cases, it can have dire implications. Aichen's lust of the eye caused him to rebel against the commandments of God. Because of this sin, God removed his hand of favor from the Israelites, and they experienced their first defeat. A simple character flaw halted the march of an entire nation into the promised land.

Similar character flaws caused the previous generation of Israelites to wander in the desert for forty years and die. They were punished for constantly rebelling against God. They struggled to reject the spirit of fear, which caused them to murmur and complain about the God who had brought them out of slavery with miracles, signs, and wonders. If character flaws are not addressed in the preparation season, they can disqualify us from obtaining out blessing. Don't let this happen to you.

While it is easy to see the flaws in other people, it is incredibly difficult to see our own flaws. It is even harder to admit our shortcomings and then do something to address them. God will allow trials to expose who we really are. Once the flaws have been identified, He desires that we address them. The trials will continue until we pass the test. Unfortunately, many of us circle our desert several times because we fail to pass the test. For those of us who can humble ourselves and submit to God's Word, obedience will enable us to continue advancing toward our destiny. As difficult as this season can be, it is designed to protect us from failing at the next level.

Imagine the pain Jerry felt being so close to his dream job only to be disqualified by a small character flaw. Worse, imagine if he got the job only to be caught later embezzling millions of dollars. Thankfully, God closed the door before Jerry's flaws would put him in jail.

If you sense that God has you in a season of preparation, stop rushing the process. Focus on what He wants you to learn. Clearly, there are some things that need to change before He will elevate you.

Warning: don't try to shortcut this process. It is critical for your future success.

Maturing the Believer

God desires to mature believers so that *overflow blessing* will not overwhelm them. In order to achieve spiritual maturity, we must study God's Word, be obedient to His Word and His will, and allow the Word to transform our lives. This will require believers to surrender their will and submit to the will of God for their lives. We must learn to walk under the guidance of the Holy Spirt and not by sight. The following verse helped me maintain the proper perspective during difficult times:

> *Consider it pure joy my brothers and sisters, whenever you face trials of many kinds, because you know that the testing of your faith produces perseverance. Let perseverance finish its work so that you may be mature and complete, not lacking anything.*
> —James 1:2-4 NIV

What are the signs of a mature believer? They have learned to manage their emotions and not be shaken by their circumstances. They possess a personal relationship with the Lord and walk in peace and love. Having endured several seasons of trials and pruning, they understand the importance of standing on God's Word and trusting Him. No longer influenced by disorder and confusion, their feet are firmly grounded in Christ Jesus. In Him, they place all their trust. Why? Because they have witnessed God's faithfulness to His children. They:

- Know they have been called according to His divine purpose.

- Have ceased leaning on their understanding and are trusting the Lord to order their footsteps.

- Are unfazed by shifting doctrine, social unrest, rumors of war, and social immorality. They have become bearers of God's grace and mercy. Everywhere they walk, people notice that something is different about them.

- Return harsh words with kindness.

- Speak life and encourage others.

- Are willing to help others and love people despite their sin.

- Are slow to anger, quick to forgive, and long suffering.

- Are gentle and kind. Their countenance oozes love and peace. When people see them, they see the love of Christ personified.

Does this describe you? Are you a mature believer?

Mature believers have learned the tactics of their Enemy. They know the attacks come at strategic times, and the purpose is to take their eyes off of God. They understand their weaknesses and how to use the Word of God to live holy lives. They are no longer slaves to fear, because they know God will provide all their needs. Daily, they put on the full armor of God before going into the marketplace to be a living witness for Christ. They understand the importance of renewing their mind daily in the Word of God. They value the power of prayer and understand the importance of listening for God's voice. Like Paul, they have learned to be content no matter the season or circumstance, because the joy of the Lord is their strength.

In contrast, immature believers struggle with trials and challenges. Pruning is foreign to them, because they are producing fruit right where they are. When things don't go their way, they are quick to mummer and complain. They love to point out the flaws of others and often possess a critical spirit. They tend to grumble about what they don't have instead of being grateful for what they do have. They are easily angered and struggle to take responsibility for their actions. Like a pine tree, the roots of their faith are very shallow. When challenging winds blow, they can be easily uprooted. They can be filled with the Word on Sunday, but empty and operating in the flesh on Monday. They do God's will as long as it does not interfere with their personal goals and desires. They prioritize their needs higher than those of others.

Immature believers evaluate things through their natural lens instead of their spiritual lens. They can be easily deceived by the Enemy to depart from God's plan for their life. They are quick to fight battles instead of allowing God to avenge them. Given these characteristics, this group tends to struggle in the season of preparation. For those who refuse to change and grow, they will forfeit their blessing and be forced to settle for much less than what God has for them.

Honestly, we all enter preparation season as immature believers. But the key is in not staying that way.

Mature believers have learned to look at life through both their natural and spiritual lenses. Instead of complaining about life events, they want to know what they are supposed to learn from the situation. They wait on God to illuminate their next steps and wait patiently for His instructions before making a move. They demonstrate spiritual maturity by not giving in to their flesh and making a move based on their emotions. They know God is the Good Shepherd, and He will take care of all who trust and obey Him.

Let's take a minute to understand what it means to be a good shepherd. In John chapter 10, Jesus describes the relationship between a shepherd and his sheep. The shepherd knows his sheep, and they recognize his voice. In the morning, he lets them out of the corral and leads them to green pastures to graze. At night, he returns them to the corral and ensures they are safe and secure. The sheep know the voice of their shepherd, and they will not follow the voice of a stranger. Jesus is our Shepherd, and the Holy Spirit is our guide. Mature believers will not stray far from His voice. The Enemy uses reasoning and deception to lead believers away from the Good Shepherd. Like a wolf, he desires to kill the dreams of the believer, to steal our joy and our peace, and to destroy our hope. This is where the real battle occurs.

Instead of trusting God to work things out, immature believers worry and make moves in their flesh. As they veer off the path God intended for them, they lose sight of their dreams and purpose. They wander aimlessly in the wilderness. Despite hard work and sacrifice, they struggle to experience the fruit of their labor. Disappointments erode their faith and drain their hope. As long as they operate in unbelief, they will wander in circles just like the Israelites did when they rejected the positive report of the two spies.

The mature believer will stand firmly on the promises of God until they see the manifestation. They will not be swayed by obstacles or setbacks. They continue standing, because they understand their faith is more precious than gold. They complete the preparation process and are ready to move to the next level.

The question for today is where do you stand in the maturation process? Are you still catering to the desires of your flesh or are you being led by your spirit man on the path to your destiny? Your answer will determine where you are in the preparation process. Remember, to whom much is given, much is required (Luke 12:48).

Finally, God is looking to see if He can trust us. If He gave us the desires of our hearts, would we continue to fellowship with Him? Would we continue to submit to His will and obey His commands? Or would we focus on trying to impress family and friends with our new blessing? Would we continue funding the activities of the kingdom, or would we pour more money into feeding our fleshly desires? Would we give God the glory for our breakthrough, or would we brag about our abilities and hard work? The real question is can God trust you to not lose your mind when He blesses you?

For me, I needed some seasons to gain control of my flesh and my tongue. Thank God for His grace and mercy, because I wasn't the fastest learner.

Have you matured in your faith? Can God trust you with an overflow blessing? Please read the next two chapters before answering that question.

Summary

God trains and equips those He has called to achieve His divine purpose. He allows situations in our lives to prepare our character, increase our level of trust, build our skills and abilities, and mature us in the faith. For those who can complete this preparation process, the overflow blessing awaits. The good news is we don't have to be good enough in our own strength. The maturing process teaches us that as we walk in faith, God will prepare us to achieve His plan for our lives. Paul wrote in 2 Corinthians 12:9 that His power is made perfect in our weakness. Thankfully, He will qualify and equip those He calls.

The parable of the talents (Matthew 25:14-30) illustrates the importance of preparing your gifts and talents. The man who received five talents was not a first-time businessman. He already had experience managing money. He was able to use the investment to scale up his existing activities, which generated additional revenues. Conversely, the person who received the one talent had not developed his gifts and skills. He did not understand business practices or usury principles. Due to his unpreparedness, his only response was to bury the talent so he would not lose it. His lack of preparation resulted in the master taking the talent from him and giving it to another person. Operating in fear will cause believers to bury their talents and miss their blessing. Don't make the same mistake.

The question is, how will you respond in this season of preparation? Will you trust God as you leave the familiar place and allow Him to prepare you to receive your blessing? Or will you forfeit your blessing because of your pride and your emotions? The fate of your destiny hangs on how you answered this question. If you choose to follow your will, you will leave the path that leads to your destiny and forfeit your blessing. Or you can choose to be obedient and continue walking down the path God has you on.

When Joseph faced this decision, he chose to trust God despite his circumstances. He allowed the process to prepare him to one day lead a powerful nation.

Will you trust the process to prepare you for your divinely appointed destiny? If this chapter has touched your spirit, then yield yourself to the tutelage of the Master Teacher. When challenging things happen, ask the simple question, *Lord, what do You want me to learn from this?* Finally, trust that everything—the good, the bad, and the ugly—is preparing you to achieve your destiny.

Remember, your overflow blessing awaits you.

Reflection Points:

1. How do you exercise your faith?

2. What have you learned from your faith challenges?

3. How does the Enemy try to distract you? Is it through the pride of life or lust of the flesh?

4. What is stopping you from moving forward in the preparation process?

5. What character flaw do you need to address?

Meditation Scriptures

Proverbs 11:2
1 John 2:16
Psalm 119:10-11
Amos 9:13 (MSG)

CHAPTER SIX

The Power of Obedience

Walk in obedience to all that the Lord your God has commanded you, so that you may live and prosper and prolong your days in the land that you will possess.

—Deuteronomy 5:33 NIV

The righteous person may have many troubles, but the Lord delivers him from them all.

—Psalm 34:19 NIV

Democracy Versus a Kingdom Government

AMERICA IS A nation that was founded when it rebelled against the King of England, George III. Our nation is a democracy, which means a government by the people involving elective representatives where the majority rules. As Americans, we value our independence and individuality. We enjoy challenging the status quo and insisting upon change. We want new menus in restaurants, new fashions in clothes, new car designs, and new cell phones. We want to have a voice in our government, our community, and our church. We believe that everyone has a voice, and it should be heard. We believe every nation should have a similar type of government. We oppose dictatorships and autocrats. With this kind of attitude, it's no wonder we struggled with the idea of being obedient to a king.

But God's government is *not* a democracy. It is a theocracy, which means a government ruled by a supreme being. The word *theocracy* can be traced back to the Greek words *theos* (a god) and *kratos* (power). In a kingdom, the king has absolute power and authority to do as he pleases. His subjects do not have input into decisions. They cannot vote on laws and principles. The king's decisions are seldom influenced by the opinions of his subjects. But a good king desires that his subjects prosper, because they reflect the effectiveness of his rulership.

In a kingdom government, God is the ultimate King, and believers are his subjects. As subjects, we have the opportunity to obey His will, His rules, and His laws. Obedience is key to experience success. The following Scripture provides keen insight for being successful in God's kingdom: *If you are willing and obedient, you shall eat the good things of the land* (Isaiah 1:19 NKJV).

The word *obedience* means the act or instance of obeying or complying with an order, request, commandment, or law. It requires submitting to a higher authority and following the commands and instructions of those in authority, independent of what one thinks or how one feels about the order.

As parents, we teach our children to obey in order to protect them, teach them self-control, and train them. Society runs in an orderly fashion because of obedience to the laws of the land. In the context of a kingdom government, it means submitting your life to the desires of the king. A good king will take care of and ensure the prosperity of his subjects, because their success (employment, security, prosperity) reflects the success of his rule.

In the case of believers, we are *in* this world, but we are not *of* this world. That is, we serve as ambassadors from the kingdom of heaven. When we proclaim Jesus Christ as our Lord and Savior, we become part of God's kingdom. We are no longer our own. We have been purchased by the blood that was shed on the cross. Consequently, as we submit to God's will for our lives, our faith matures, and He reveals more of His glorious nature. As His will becomes our will, we begin to desire the things He wanted to give us in the first place. With that said, let's take a deeper dive into how a kingdom government operates.

In his book *Kingdom Principles*, Dr. Myles Monroe states that there is no such thing as private property in a kingdom. Everything belongs to the king. Anything that one uses in the kingdom is a privilege granted by the king. Submission to the lordship of the king means that we forgo our individual right to our lives. Again, in the case of Christians, the moment we confess Jesus as Lord, we grant Him sovereign control over our lives. Our obedience to His will signifies that He is both Lord and Savior. Here are a few principles Dr. Monroe shares with his readers about operating in a kingdom:

- *Kingship has to do with authority; lordship has to do with ownership.*

- *There is no such thing as lordship without obedience.*

- *Jesus is either Lord of all, or He is not Lord at all.*

- *In the kingdom of heaven, there is no economic crisis, and there are no shortages.*

- *Relinquishing ownership puts us in the position of full access to all of heaven's resources.*

In order to thrive in a theocracy, one must explicitly obey the king. In God's kingdom, we have to obey His Word, which we have in the form of the Bible. Unlike a democracy, we do not have a vote in God's kingdom. Rather, He is looking for trustworthy subjects through whom He can release heaven into the earth—those who are faithfully committed to serving independent of personal desires or needs.

This can be a stumbling block for believers who possess strong personalities and are fiercely independent. It may require staying in the season of preparation longer than others in order to break the spirit of rebellion. But learning to carry our cross daily will be crucial to staying in the perfect will of God. God is not going to come against our free will. He will allow us to circle the desert several times until we are willing to follow His plan. Those who desire an overflow blessing will choose to obey and trust God as they walk toward their destiny.

The question for today is "will you choose to be obedient to His will?"

The Best for His Children

When we were created, God planted seeds deep within us that would enable us to achieve our destiny. As we experience life, these seeds blossom and bloom. With careful cultivation and nurturing, they will eventually produce fruit. Then He prunes us so we will produce *much* fruit. Soon, our lives become a neon sign glorifying His name and power. People are receptive of our testimony because of the Christ they see in us. Yes, our Father loves His children.

Since He is a good father, God promises to guide us through life situations. Psalm 128:1 says, *Blessed are all who fear the Lord, who walk in obedience to Him* (NIV). Here, the word *fear* means to have reverence for the Lord, which means that instead of stumbling through life on our own strength and intelligence, we can be obedient to the Lord, who then guides our steps. Instead of wondering about our purpose, we can obey and walk in it daily. This will require shifting our focus from self to God. Christian author Max Lucado says it best in his book *Facing Your Giant*: "When we focus on our giants, we stumble, but when we focus on God, our giants will tumble." Can the church say amen?

Obedience Creates Opportunities

The key to being successful is focusing on today and executing in the now, because success breeds success. Opportunities abound for successful people. Opportunity providers will look at a track record of a successful person (otherwise known as a resume) and assume the person will be successful again. They understand that success requires obedience to delivering results that exceed expectations.

Unfortunately, some people focus more on chasing new opportunities rather than excelling in their current assignment. When they deliver average results, they don't understand why they are not getting better assignments.

The lesson for modern believers is not to become fixated on walking in our destiny. We should focus on excelling in our daily assignments. When we study the story of Joseph, we see that God's favor was upon the young man in all he did. So, how did his obedience translate into new opportunity?

Joseph's world was shattered by his brothers' cruel act of vengeance. As the shock wore off, Joseph found himself far away from everything he knew and loved. His destiny stood beyond the western horizon in a distant, foreign land. Imagine the grief and anger he must have experienced when his freedom was torn away. But his actions reveal the secret to his success. Instead of rebelling against his enslavement, Joseph embraced the opportunities presented to him at Potiphar's house. His obedience enabled him to be successful despite being a slave. Genesis 39:2-4 tells us that the Lord was with Joseph and gave him success in everything he did. Potiphar recognized that the Lord was with Joseph and made him his personal attendant.

What did Potiphar see in Joseph that was different from the other slaves? He saw a slave working with a positive attitude. He saw a young boy who was a quick learner and completed his work in excellence. He saw a slave who actually had good ideas and was capable of making things better. He saw someone with the gift of organizing work and getting things done efficiently. Unlike other slaves who begrudgingly completed their tasks with marginal success, everything Joseph touched was successful, to the point that he prospered in the house of Potiphar.

What was the secret to Joseph's success? The answer can be found in Psalm 37:23 which says, *The steps of a good man are ordered by the Lord and He delights in his ways* (NKJV). By choosing to obey and do the will of his master, Joseph honored the Lord in his daily actions. God rewarded Joseph's faithfulness by allowing His favor to rest upon him. To understand the impact of God's favor, let's take a look at Joseph's background.

Joseph and his family lived a nomadic way of life as livestock herders. Their skills and experiences were better suited for living in the open plains rather than running a large household. The chores of a domesticated slave were quite foreign to Joseph. But because of his obedience and commitment to the work at hand, God's favor enabled him to be successful. God showed him what to do and how to do it. Notice that people were not impressed by Joseph's skills and knowledge. They saw that it was the Lord who made Joseph successful.

How did these people know it was the Lord? Because Joseph shared with them the source that enabled him to have success. In his obedience, Joseph was glorifying God. Even though Joseph was blessed in his master's house, that was not the overflow blessing.

When Joseph was thrown into the king's prison, he experienced a similar level of success. Because of his obedience, the Lord guided his actions and granted him favor with the prison warden. Soon, Joseph was in charge of all those held in prison and responsible for the daily operations. The Bible says the warden trusted Joseph because the Lord was with him, and he was successful in whatever he did (Genesis 39:20-23). Again, Joseph's success was not attributed to his skills. They were attributed to the hand of God that was upon Joseph's life. While Joseph was blessed in the prison, that was still not the overflow blessing.

In each situation, Joseph's obedience earned him the trust of his masters. They rewarded Joseph by giving him more opportunities with greater levels of responsibility. The favor of the Lord ensured that he was successful beyond man's ability to comprehend. Instead of focusing on the negative aspects of his condition, Joseph poured all his energy into his work. Instead of complaining about his circumstances, he faithfully executed the work assigned to him. Because of his faithfulness, he was entrusted to manage both Potiphar's house and the prison, even though he was still in bondage. Jesus spoke to his disciples about this principle in the parable of the shrewd manager.

Whoever can be trusted with very little can also be trusted with much and whoever is dishonest with very little will be dishonest with much. So, if you have not been trustworthy in handling worldly wealth, who will trust you with true riches?
—Luke 16:10-11 NIV

I remember having several discussions with young engineers during the annual performance review process. They complained about not getting high visibility projects that would position them for a promotion. In each case, as we reviewed their performance for the year, there were some aspects below the company's expectations. For some, they had been late several times with their monthly reports and struggled to hit deadlines. For others, feedback from their production customers indicated they were habitually late to meetings and had poor troubleshooting skills. My feedback to them was blunt and straight to the point. "If you want to have more opportunities, be successful in the ones you have now. Stop worrying about the future, and focus on succeeding in the present."

When Joseph was in Potiphar's house, he didn't focus on the dream God gave him. He focused on doing the work at hand and being obedient to God's direction.

Are you being obedient in your current assignment?

Obedience Glorifies God

To glorify God means to extol His attributes such as holiness, faithfulness, grace, mercy, love, compassion, comfort, and peace, just to name a few. It means to bestow honor, to praise, or to worship God. When we glorify God through our obedience, we represent as admirable His will for our lives. When we are obedient to God's commandments, we walk upright in righteousness. Our obedience reflects the Word hidden in our hearts. It reflects our daily relationship with the Father. Our words and actions reflect His plan for our lives. As a sweet consequence, we become walking testimonies of His glory and power.

The fruit produced from our obedience to His will brings God glory. When our actions and behaviors align with His Word, people see the God of the person. All God is looking for is a vessel of honor, one who will submit to the leading of the Holy Spirit. The Apostle Paul wrote, *so whether you eat or drink or whatever you do, do it all for the glory of God* (1 Corinthians 10:31 NIV).

The secret to being obedient is trusting the Lord's purpose for our lives and learning to rest in that knowledge. It will come to pass not by our strength, but by His power. The question is what kind of fruit are we producing in our daily lives? *In the same way, let your light shine before others, that they may see your good deeds and glorify your father in heaven* (Matthew 5:16 NIV).

How many of us are glorifying God in our jobs, our marriages, or in our church? When people look at us, who do they see? Do they see the Christ in us, or do they see our self-centered flesh? The answer can be found in this simple question: who is Lord in your life? If we are not willing to crucify our flesh daily, it is not the Lord. Obedience requires sacrifice. We must be willing to sacrifice our desires and our vision to obey the voice of the Father. Who better knows what we want or need than our Creator?

Jesus understood His mission on the earth was to do the will of God. When Jesus was twelve years old, his family traveled to Jerusalem for the annual Feast of the Passover. When they left to return home, his parents did not notice that Jesus was missing. After they had traveled one day's distance from town, only then did they realize He was missing. They frantically searched for Him for three days. They finally found Him in the temple where He was listening to the teachers and asking them questions. When they asked what had happened to Him, Jesus responded, *Why did you seek me? Did you not know that I must be about My Father's business?* (Luke 2:49 NKJV).

How many of us are about our Father's business? Who of us has decided to forego personal will and seek God's will for our lives? Jesus did.

Early in life, Jesus understood His purpose and the importance of timing. Although He was obedient to His earthly parents, Jesus was also obedient to His heavenly Father. When his mother asked him to turn water into wine for the wedding feast, He told her it wasn't His time yet. Nevertheless, He obeyed his earthly mother and complied with her request. During the three years of His earthly ministry, He walked in obedience to God's will. On several occasions, He told those around Him He could only do what His Father commanded. He knew that completing each assignment would glorify His Father to the world. On the night He was betrayed, Jesus spoke the following words that illustrate this point.

After Jesus said this, he looked toward heaven and prayed:

"Father, the hour has come. Glorify your Son, that your Son may glorify you. For you granted him authority over all people that he might give eternal life to all those you have given him. Now this is eternal life: that they may know you, the only true God, and Jesus Christ, whom you have sent. I have brought you glory on earth by finishing the work you gave me to do. And now, Father, glorify me in your presence with the glory I had with you before the world began."

—John 17:1-5 NIV

His death on the cross would be the ultimate sacrifice for the sins of the world. Because of His obedience, billions of souls would come to know the Lord and be saved. And His obedience was acknowledged by His father who said in Matthew 17:5, *This is my son, whom I love; with him I am well pleased* (NIV).

What will God say about your actions? Will your obedience please Him? If this has pricked your spirit, maybe it's time to make some changes.

Obedience Strengthens the Weak

Staying in a place of obedience will stretch our faith and strengthen our resilience, because we cannot see or comprehend what God wants to do in our lives. The Bible says His thoughts are not our thoughts, and His ways are not our ways (Isaiah 55:8). We have to walk a path we can't see except for the one step He has illuminated. Thankfully, He promises not to give us more than we can endure.

As we focus on God, He promises to increase our ability to persevere, because the testing of our faith has a divine purpose, which is to develop patience and trust in the Lord. The testing brings about the maturation of the believer. Obedience also allows us to tap into the power of God. Isaiah 40:29 says, *He gives strength to the weary and increases the power of the weak* (NIV).

In his second letter to the church in Corinth, Paul shared that the disciples had been under great pressure (due to persecution) during their time in the providence of Asia Minor (2 Corinthians 1:7-9). Things were so bad, they lost hope in life itself. Yet they survived due to the God who both delivered and strengthened them. Paul said this season of extreme testing taught them to rely solely on God. Because God had delivered them from deadly perils before, Paul was confident He would do it again.

Confidence is a characteristic that cannot be taught or given. It has to be earned from enduring hardships and overcoming obstacles.

Confidence is built when we face challenges and are not overwhelmed by them. I found the following quote by Rod Parsley while surfing the internet one day: "We draw our strength from the battle. From our greatest conflicts come our greatest victories!"

The writers of the gospels chronicled the life of an exemplary citizen, Jesus. When Jesus was on earth, He provided many examples of how to live and prosper as an obedient kingdom citizen. Although He walked on earth with the spiritual authority He had in heaven, He chose obedience to the will of the Father over His personal desires. Luke 4:1-13 describes the temptation of Jesus by the Enemy.

After Jesus was baptized by John the Baptist, He went into the desert where he fasted for forty days. During this time, Satan tempted Him three times to operate in pride for personal gain. Jesus overcame each one by quoting Scripture. When Satan withdrew in defeat, the angels ministered to the needs of Jesus.

This story provides us with key insights on how to stand in the face of difficult trials. The first point is learning to crucify our flesh in order to stay in the will of God. Certainly, Jesus had the power to make bread and satisfy His hunger. He could have stepped off of the top of the temple and been saved by the heavenly host. But those things were not in the perfect will of God. By choosing to be obedient to the will of God, Jesus left us with a powerful example of how we can walk in victory.

The second point is that we must stand on the Word of God during our tests and trials. In order to stand on the Word, we must first know the Word and then obey it. When we do this in faith, we tap into His power, for His power is made perfect in our weakness (2 Corinthians 12:9). The simple act of obedience is critical for walking in victory every day.

Obedience Releases Resources

When God wants us to do something, He will ensure we have everything to complete the assignment. This principle can be seen when Joseph volunteered to interpret the dreams of Pharaoh's officials, the cup bearer, and chief baker. Both had angered Pharaoh and were subsequently thrown into prison. There, the captain of the guard assigned Joseph to take care of them. After they had been there a while, they both had different dreams on the same night. When Joseph saw them the next day, they looked dejected. They told him they had dreams but there was no one to interpret them. Joseph responded that the interpretations belonged to God and asked them to share their dreams. Each man told Joseph his dream, and Joseph interpreted each accordingly.

How did Joseph know God interprets dreams? Why was he confident to explain their dreams? This kind of confidence is impossible unless Joseph had learned to place his trust in the God of the universe—trust that was developed over time by being obedient to God's leading. The God who told Joseph how to be successful in prison and at Potiphar's house, told him the meaning of the dreams. The same God wants to show you how to be successful on the path toward your destiny.

As we walk down the path for our lives, we will find ourselves in situations we cannot achieve with our natural abilities. This is where God will honor our obedience and enable us to complete our trials and tests. When we are obedient to the will of God, we can access the power of God. He will give us everything we need to complete His will for our lives. When He adds His *super* to our *natural*, unknown things become known, and the impossible become possible. Joseph's simple act of obedience allowed him to operate in the favor of God. Because he trusted God, God showed him what to do, how to do it, and when to do it.

No matter what you are facing, God wants to guide you through it. Just trust in Him and obey.

Here are some simple truths from Joseph's story:

- How did Joseph learn how to run a complex household? GOD!

- How did he learn how to run the king's jail? GOD!

- How did he learn how to interpret dreams? GOD!

- How will you achieve your vision? GOD!

- How will you reach the overflow blessing? GOD!

There are so many benefits from walking in obedience. Walking in continued obedience to His Word and His voice allows us to experience God's power. Obedience facilitates the maturing of our faith. It creates discipline and teaches us to trust. It helps create focus and minimizes the impact of distractions. Obedience signals the Father that we are ready to receive more of His glory. It frees us from the stress of finding our purpose. Obedience places responsibility on God to achieve our final destination. In retrospect, the path to the overflow blessing will create a powerful testimony that glorifies God and changes lives.

Let me address a common misconception. God does not select people to receive an overflow blessing based on their skills and abilities. Rather, He looks at their heart and their willingness to be obedient.

God is looking to be glorified by His plan for your life, not your skills and knowledge. That is why he exalts the humble and opposes the proud. He knows the humble will not try to claim His glory. Stop worrying. Focus on obeying the last set of instructions you received. Trust that God will guide you forward as you walk out your destiny.

Staying on the Right Path

Before the invention of the GPS, people depended on physical maps to determine the best route to get from point A to point B. Companies such as AAA specialized in mapping out interstate routes for drivers wanting to explore America.

My parents once received a map with certain routes highlighted in yellow for our upcoming vacation. They diligently followed the path highlighted on the map to reach our vacation spot. In a similar fashion, God wants to illuminate the path for our lives. Finding the first step on the path will require us to be obedient to the leading of the Holy Spirit.

While God will give us a glimpse of our future, finding the path that takes us there will require obedience and walking by faith. As we begin moving toward the vision, God reveals the steps He wants us to travel.

Take King David, for instance. His journey from being anointed by Samuel to actually being crowned king of Israel involved a lengthy period of time running from the wrath of Saul. While caves and foreign lands were a long way from the promised kingship, David continued to trust God. In Psalm 16, David praises God for providing him with refuge, counseling, provision, and strength. He says, *You will show me the path of life. In Your presence is fullness of joy; At Your right hand are pleasures forevermore* (vs. 11 NKJV).

David understood the connection between obedience and staying on the path of life. Growing up as a shepherd boy, he learned to depend on God for everything. This knowledge enabled him to survive attacks by wild animals and mocking giants. The time he spent hiding from Saul reinforced the importance of being obedient to God. Admittedly, David struggled with the desires of his flesh, and this often got him in trouble. That being said, David is best remembered for valuing his relationship with God.

Obedience means ignoring the desires of the flesh in order to follow the will of God. Sometimes it means not listening to the advice of friends whose good intentions counter what God is saying. Sometimes it means walking alone for a season, because no one can see where God is taking you. Instead of worrying about finding the next step, let's learn from David and cast our attention on the Lord. *Show me your ways, Lord, teach me your paths* (Psalm 25:4 NIV).

In her book *Just Enough Light for the Step I Am On*, Stormie Omartian talks about God revealing the steps we are to take as we walk by faith. She contends that many people wait for God to reveal the steps *before* they will move. Though this waiting on God seems to make sense before making a move, it does not align with His Word. The Bible says that *faith without works is dead* (James 2:20 KJV). It is not enough to believe. We have to put some action behind our beliefs.

Believers who wait for revelation before moving don't get very far, because God waits on them to move by faith before He releases more revelation. The truth is you have to be willing to go out and knock on a few doors before God reveals the one He has for you. Omartian encourages readers to pray that God will close any door He does not want them to enter, leaving open only the door He wants His children to enter.

Stop waiting on God. Start knocking on some doors, and trust Him to show you the one you are supposed to enter.

If there are paths that lead to life, there must be paths that lead to death and destruction, such as fulfilling carnal desires as warned in Proverbs 22:5. *In the paths of the wicked are snares and pitfalls, but those who would preserve their life stay far from them* (NIV). These snares and pitfalls are carnal desires that are meant to distract people from achieving their God-given destiny. Be mindful of distractions and things that seem good. Everything that glitters is not gold.

Jesus taught on this topic in the parable of the prodigal son (Luke 15:11-32). Here, the word *prodigal* means to spend money or resources freely, lavishly, wastefully, or extravagantly.

In the story, the youngest son is captivated by the thought of being out on his own, away from the rules of his father. After receiving his share of the family estate, he runs off to a distant land where he squanders his fortune on wild living. He soon finds himself broke and forced to work for other men to survive. As he struggles to find something to eat, the words of his father ring in his ears: a warning about chasing carnal paths that lead to traps designed to divert the runner from the path of life. But the son—who wanted to see the world and make his own decisions—finds himself eating what the pigs are eating. If he would have only listened to the wise council of his father.

How many of us have ignored the advice of friends and family, and chosen paths that took us away from our destiny? Paths that took us to dead ends and caused us to experience delays in achieving our destiny. When the lost son came to his senses, he returned home where he was welcomed by his father. God wants to do the same thing for His wayward sons and daughters. All we have to do is to turn around and choose to walk on the path God highlights for us.

If you are mourning because you ended up on a dead end, make a U-turn, and allow God to guide you back on His path for your life.

Passing Our Test

God periodically gives us tests to determine the quality of our character. How we respond reveals the depth of our spiritual growth and how far we need to go. The testing reveals and illuminates the nature of our hearts and what is contained therein. God wants us to pass the tests before He allows us to go to the next part of our journey. James 1:2 states:

Consider it pure joy my brothers and sisters, whenever you face trials of many kinds, because you know that the testing of your faith produces perseverance. Let perseverance finish its work so that you may be mature and complete, not lacking anything. (NIV)

In the simplest of terms, do not fret about the challenges you face. Some of them are tests in disguise.

In 1 Samuel chapter 24, Saul was returning from chasing the Philistines when he received news that David was in the desert of En Gedi. Saul took 3000 men and went searching for him. One fateful day, Saul entered a cave to relieve himself. Hidden deep in the cave was David and some of his men. When his men saw Saul, they told David, *This is the day the Lord spoke of when he said "I will give your enemy into your hands for you to deal with as you wish." David crept up unnoticed and cut off a corner of Saul's robe* (vs. 4).

Afterward, David felt conviction for touching the Lord's anointed. One might argue that David had every reason to kill Saul, who had chased him across Israel with the intention of killing him. If anyone had a reason to harm Saul it was David. But David feared the Lord more than getting his revenge. He knew not to touch what God had ordained. Later, he would write in Psalm 105:15, *Touch not mine anointed, and do my prophets no harm* (KJV). This simple act of self-control reflected David's obedience to God's will. I wonder how many of us could pass the twenty-first century version of that test?

Several years ago, I had an incident that tested my obedience to this Scripture. While I was at rehearsal with the church's praise team, I had a negative encounter with one of the ministers. He came at me with loud verbal insults to express his dissatisfaction with me and my work as the team's keyboardist. It was so loud and intense, I thought there would be a physical altercation. By the grace of God, I was able to stay calm and not respond.

Fortunately, I remembered the story of David. I knew not to touch God's anointed and match verbal assault with verbal assault. By chance, another minister walked into the sanctuary and witnessed the whole scenario. He confirmed that I did not do anything to precipitate the incident. The next day, I had a message from the minister who assaulted me indicating he wanted to talk to me.

Now, here was my test. Would I respond with forgiveness, or was

I going to allow my anger to influence how I would respond? With the latter, I certainly would have flunked the test. Yes, I was mad as heck, and I did not want to play for the praise team anymore. Thank goodness for the Holy Spirit who convicted me to do the right thing. After much prayer, I returned the call, and we talked. He shared his concerns with me and apologized for his behavior. My response surprised me. I gracefully accepted his apology and continued to play for the praise team.

Afterward, I realized the incident was just a test to see if I would obey God's Word. During a moment of reflection on my assailant's feedback, God revealed some things I needed to change about my own behavior. In the end, God used that situation to teach both of us about our weaknesses and our dependence on Him. Additionally, God healed my pain and restored our friendship.

The simple secret to passing God's test is being obedient to His Word. This will require reading and memorizing Scripture. You will not experience the victory if you are a hearer of the Word only. You must be a doer and put the Word into action in order to see the fruition. If you fail a test, don't fret. You will have an opportunity to take it again. Just like school, you cannot advance to the next level until you pass your test.

Don't get angry with God when things are not progressing in your life. He might be waiting on you to pass the anger test before He will bring you that promotion opportunity.

Disobedience Delays the Vision

The story of Jericho highlights both the power of obedience and the price of disobedience (Joshua 6). When Moses died, Joshua led the Israelites across the Jordan river and into the promised land. This group had grown up depending on God's provision. All they knew was obedience to God's instructions, and they trusted Him explicitly.

Regardless of how difficult, illogical, or silly the instructions, this generation of Israelites knew to obey the God of Abraham.

When they came to the city of Jericho, God instructed the Israelites to walk around the city for six days in total silence. How did they do that? Imagine trying to organize even 100 people to walk around a city for one entire day and not make a sound. This story illustrates the power of unity. Such was the discipline of the Israelites that hundreds of thousands of people obeyed the commands.

For six days, their silence reflected the reverence they had for God as they circled the walled city. Because of their obedience, God moved in His power on the seventh day to deliver the city to them. The people were instructed to destroy everything and to turn the spoils of the treasury over to the Lord. There was jubilance in the camp because God had delivered their first victory. Confidence was high, and people were joyous with excitement.

Unfortunately, this is where the story turns because of a simple act of disobedience (Joshua 7). One person sinned by stealing some of the loot and burying it near his tent. A short time later, the Israelites tasted defeat when the men of Ai routed the Israelite scouting party. News of this setback quickly demoralized the people and their leaders. When Joshua inquired of the Lord, he questioned why God had allowed them to be defeated by their enemies. The Lord responded that Israel had violated His commands, and they would not prevail until the sin had been identified and addressed. Specifically, the Lord said:

I will not be with you anymore unless you destroy whatever among you is devoted to destruction. Go, consecrate the people. Tell them, "Consecrate yourselves in preparation for tomorrow; for this is what the Lord, the God of Israel, says: 'There are devoted things among you, Israel. You cannot stand against your enemies until you remove them.

—Joshua 7:12-13 NIV

Next, the Lord instructed Joshua to go through all the tribes until he found the origin of the sin. With God's guidance, Joshua was able to identify Achan (out of hundreds of thousands of people) as the source of the sin. When Joshua confronted Achan, he admitted taking some of the devoted things himself. Once the items were recovered, Joshua's judgment was swift and severe. Then God instructed Joshua to attack the city of Ai. This time, He enabled the Israelites to be victorious over the people of Ai. A simple act of disobedience halted the nation from claiming God's promise. When the Israelites fell outside of God's plan, God removed His power, which resulted in defeat for the Israelites.

Remember, God's power always accompanies God's will. Who does this statement apply to? *Why do you call me "Lord, Lord," and do not do what I say?* (Luke 6:46 NIV).

Disobedience stops movement toward God's vision for our lives. It will cause us to diverge from the path God has for us, delaying progress toward the vision. Leaving the path will cost us wasted time and energy as well as rob us of our peace. Disobedience will cause us to struggle in our own strength, all because we did not want to obey God.

Imagine driving across the country and not following the instructions of your GPS system. While you may eventually get to your destination, it will not be by the shortest route. Disobedience causes people to forfeit their blessing. It caused the Israelites to wander in the desert for forty years. It cost Saul his kingship. It caused Moses to not enter the promised land. How many people are blaming the Enemy for blocking their path when, in reality, it was a simple act of disobedience that took them out of the will of God. Do not allow disobedience to cause you to miss your destiny.

Summary

Our Father has wonderful plans for our lives. He promises to guide us along the path of life to reach our destiny and His divine blessings. Like any father, God desires obedience from His children. The Bible says He will guide us on the steps we should take. The only thing we have to do is obey His commands and operate by faith.

The Bible is full of great men and women who were obedient to God's Word and His voice. Their stories encourage and inspire modern believers to persevere through trials and tests, because we trust God to order our steps. There is no need to guess what we should be doing. All we have to do is allow the Holy Spirit to lead/ direct us and obey.

In 1887, John Sammis wrote a Christian hymn titled "Trust and Obey." We sang this song often when I attended church in Wilmington NC. The words resonated in my spirit long after the last time I sang that song, because it was a powerful reminder of how to have a victorious life. "Trust and obey, for there's no other way. To be happy with Jesus, but to trust and obey." I pray these words resonate with your spirit today.

While it sounds so simple to do in theory, this tends to be a major stumbling block for believers. The battle between the flesh and the spirit rages daily, and the victor will determine who we will obey. This is the purpose of trials and testing. They give us opportunities to strengthen our spirit man and to subdue the carnal nature. Why? Because the carnal man will always reject the things of God, because he is too focused on satisfying his desires. The trials teach us to obey God's Word which, in turn, results in us trusting Him more.

All of the great biblical figures experienced the power of obedience. Moses spent forty years training in the desert to obey God. Joshua led the people into the promised land, because he obeyed God. Obedience enabled Deborah and Barak to experience victory over the Sisera and Canaanite army. The stories of Able, Enoch, Noah,

Abraham, Isaac, Joseph, Gideon, and Rahab remind us of the importance of obeying God's instruction.

Obedience produce a wealth of fruit such as righteousness, integrity, trustworthiness, and humility. Obedience opens the door to access God's favor and blessings. Obedience will protect you from distractions and counterfeit opportunities. It teaches us to rest in the perfect will of God. It will minimize delays and shield us from the deceptive practices of the Enemy.

That being said, disobedience will take us out of the will of the Father. It can cause us to forfeit the vision God has for us (Saul) and open the door for judgment (Eli's sons). It will disqualify you from tapping into God's provision and power and force you to operate in your own strength. If this chapter resonated with your spirit, maybe it's time to re-align yourself by confessing your errors and requesting guidance to get back on the right path.

Heavenly Father,
Forgive me for not aligning to your will.
I am tired of trying to do things my way.
You know the plans you have for me.
Plans to prosper and not harm me.
Align me back on your path.
Guide me back to the path of life.
In Jesus name I pray,
Amen

Reflection Points:

1. Is Jesus the Lord of your life? If so, what areas in your life have you surrendered to Him?

2. How do you crucify your flesh daily?

3. When God gives you instructions, do you obey immediately?

4. What is hindering you from obeying God's will?

5. What happens when you try to move independent of God?

Meditation Scriptures:

Isaiah 1:19
Proverbs 22:4
Psalm 25:4
Psalm 16:11
Psalm 119:105
Psalm 34:1

CHAPTER SEVEN

Managing the Emotional Roller Coaster

We demolish arguments and every pretension that sets itself up against the knowledge of God, and we take captive every thought to make it obedient to Christ.

—2 Corinthians 10:5 NIV

THE JOURNEY BETWEEN the revelation of what's to come and the manifestation is full of successes, setbacks, and disappointments. During this time, our emotions will ricochet all over the place, depending on our thinking.

In many ways, this journey is similar to riding a roller coaster. The ups and downs correspond to the successes and challenges of life. How we respond emotionally can significantly impact achieving our destiny (i.e. the revelation). From the excitement associated with the revelation of the vision to the uncertainty associated with navigating through the challenges on the way to achieving destiny, our emotions will be thoroughly exercised before reaching our destination.

Failing to manage our emotions will cause us to abandon the path to the overflow blessing. Our emotions can open the door to justifying our flesh-centered actions. Ultimately, this will lead us to disobey

God's instructions and wander in the wilderness for a season. When we lack control over our emotions, they make it difficult to sacrifice our will for God's plans.

In more than twenty years of being a people manager, I have witnessed the negative consequences resulting from employees failing to manage their emotions. Untimely emotional outbursts have cost people valued relationships and missed opportunities. This is an area many believers, including myself, struggle with. Thankfully, God's patience is infinite because some of us (okay, me especially) have definitely exceeded our allotment. Managing our emotions will be critical for achieving our God-given destiny. The story of Joseph provided me with keen insight into controlling my emotions.

After reading Joseph's story several times, I finally noticed the absence of negative emotions. This led me to question how he managed his feelings through those difficult times. Let's face it, Joseph had a right to be angry and bitter. He had been robbed of his freedom by vengeful brothers who sold him into slavery. He was falsely accused by Potiphar's wife and thrown into Pharaoh's jail. He had been forgotten by Pharaoh's cup bearer when he was released. Despite these setbacks, Joseph's behavior indicates that not only did he accept his circumstance, he also transformed every problem into an achievement.

- How did he stay so calm and focused?

- How was he able to thrive in a place where he did not want to be?

- How was he able to have joy and peace?

The process that prepares believers to receive God's blessing will strain and pull our emotions all over the place. In the beginning, there is excitement over the revelation of the vision. For Joseph, this was the dream God gave him. Moving out of the comfortable place may leave us frustrated and confused. For Joseph, this was his brothers selling him into slavery. While we are being prepared in the wilderness period, our fears are uncovered and addressed, our character is refined, and our skill set expanded. This was Joseph's time in slavery and prison.

Our obedience during the wilderness period will enable us to overcome anger and disappointment. But one of the secrets to persevering through these phases is learning how to manage our emotions. It's okay to experience the range of emotions, but we cannot allow them to dictate our actions. God has a plan for us, and we are on a mission. We cannot allow emotions to rule our behavior.

Controlling Your Emotions

Emotions play a critical role for humans by providing visual cues about our state of being. At a glance, you can tell if someone is happy, sad, angry, frustrated, confused, or lost. Our emotions reflect our mental state, which can influence our thoughts. When we receive and process information, our emotions convey how the input made us feel.

For example, when things happen that we perceive to be negative, it is reflected in our emotions. This can be either a good thing or a bad thing, depending on how we respond. In order to successfully navigate the preparation process, we must learn to control our emotions and not be ruled by them. Being obedient to God's will can conflict with our personal desires. When this happens, we must be careful how we respond, because negative emotions can lead to undesirable consequences.

One Saturday in 1969, my father took my brother and me downtown to the Sears Department Store. This store had a beautiful candy kiosk filled with all kinds of yummy goodies. When we passed the kiosk, a wonderful treat caught my brother's eye. The normally quiet sibling begged and pleaded with Dad to get him some candy. When dad told him no, he lost it. Right in front of everyone, my brother flung his little body to the floor, making sure he faced upward so Dad could see him. With every bit of energy he could muster, he kicked and screamed, cried, then kicked and screamed some more. I bent down and pulled on his arm to get him up, but he would not budge.

Everyone was looking at us. The next thing I saw was a blur as Dad snatched him off the floor and proceeded to remind him who was in charge (during this time, public spankings were accepted—unruly kids were not). Instead of swaying dad to get some candy, my brother's emotional outburst caused him to experience extreme pain. If only he had listened to me.

Spoken words have the power to set things in motion. Words spoken from an emotional state can have dire consequences. Dad's response to my brother's temper tantrum taught me a valuable lesson about controlling my emotions. While it is okay to feel a certain way about a situation, we need to focus on doing the right thing regardless. In other words, we need to have control over our emotions. Unchecked, our emotions can make a negative situation worse.

Going back to Joseph's story, he would not have been successful in Potiphar's house if he would have allowed himself to be consumed by anger and frustration. If Joseph had been consumed by bitterness towards Potiphar's wife, he would not have been in position to interpret the dreams of Pharaoh's official. If Joseph had not been able to forgive his brothers, the hope for the nation of Israel would have perished during the famine. The point is great people do not allow their emotions to cloud their decisions/actions.

In March of 1865, President Abraham Lincoln was inaugurated for his second term in office. The Civil War was entering the final phase, and victory was in sight. This bloody conflict had torn the nation apart and claimed the lives of over 600,000 Americans. In his speech to the nation, Lincoln laid the framework for reuniting the country. Instead of allowing anger and vindictiveness to taint the eye of the victors, Lincoln's message focused on healing the nation's wounds.

With malice toward none, with charity for all, with firmness in the right, as God gives us to see the right, let us strive on to finish the work we are in, to bind up the nation's wounds.

—Abraham Lincoln

Though Lincoln called for peace, his message conflicted with the views held by several members of his war cabinet and Congress. They wanted to make the South pay for their treason. But Lincoln's focus shifted from prosecuting a war to laying the foundation for healing the nation. After the fall of Richmond several weeks later, Lincoln met with the North's General Ulysses S. Grant to discuss surrender terms. He shared his desire to begin the reconciliation of the divided land. With the war winding down quickly, a series of defeats prompted Confederate General Robert E. Lee to request a meeting with Grant to discuss terms of surrender. When Grant met Lee at the Appomattox courthouse on April 9th, Grant agreed to pardon Confederate soldiers and officers.

As the Confederate soldiers marched past the Union troops to surrender their firearms, the Union troops rendered honors to their fellow Americans. Instead of taunting their former enemies, the soldiers stood at attention in silence. This sign of respect signaled the beginning of the reconciliation process. The first seeds were sown to bring about the healing of the nation.

Lincoln's response reflected the belief that his mission was to preserve the nation. This mission superseded any negative emotions he may have felt toward his Southern brothers. He could not allow his feelings to distract him from completing his mission.

In similar fashion, we must control our emotions while we are being prepared for the overflow blessing in order to reach our destiny. That means learning to have peace no matter the situation or circumstances we find ourselves in. Out of all the New Testament prophets (except the Lord, of course) I think the apostle Paul understood the importance of managing emotions. Through the many trials he faced with the disciples, Paul found that focusing on Christ enabled him to weather every storm. *I have learned the secret of being content in any and every situation, whether well fed or hungry, whether living in plenty or in want* (Philippians 4:12 NIV).

I want to encourage my readers to refrain from allowing emotions to disqualify you from receiving all God has in store.

Emotions will cause us to complain about challenges that are designed to strengthen and improve us. When we react, we run the risk of damaging key relationships, closing open doors, and sealing future doors shut. When we sense our emotions trying to wreck God's plan, we need to bind them up with faith until they come in line with God's plan. Otherwise, chaos is the result.

Take Saul, for example. Anxiety caused him to be a people pleaser. He lost his kingdom when he chose to appease the people rather than obey God. Fear almost cost Moses his life. Pride caused Absalom to lead a revolt against David's kingship. Depression drove Elijah to the brink of giving up.

Consequently, the lesson is not to let our emotions disqualify us from finishing the race and receiving our prize.

The Power of a Positive Attitude

Maintaining a positive attitude is crucial for being successful in life. Your perspective on life plays a significant part in achieving your vision. People who see the glass as half full tend to view life through optimistic lenses. They believe in positive outcomes from every situation. They view problems as opportunities waiting on solutions.

Those who see the glass as half empty tend to have a pessimistic view of life. They gravitate toward worrying about the unknowns and tend to respond negatively to new challenges.

The Bible says as a man thinks in his heart, so is he (Proverbs 23:7). Our thoughts govern our actions and behaviors. We are the sum of all our thoughts and feelings. In the armories of our mind are forged the tools that create either our successes or our failures. It is imperative that we protect what we allow our minds to be exposed to. We must cast down negative thoughts and bring them into the captivity of Christ (2 Corinthians 10:5). We need to protect our eye and ear gates from negative conversations, distractions and anything that inspires fear or doubt. Zig Ziglar says, "Doubt kills more dreams than failure ever will."

The old adage "the best defense is a good offence" justifies why believers need to meditate on the Word of God daily. When we make a habit of starting our day with reading and praying, we apply the armor of God that will enable us to stand (Ephesian 6:10-18). When we speak about our day, our words put things into motion that bring about the manifestation. When we renew our minds daily by studying the Word of God, we can hear His voice better, which allows us to walk in His will.

Do not conform to the pattern of this world, but be transformed by the renewing of your mind. Then you will be able to test and approve what God's will is – his good, pleasing and perfect will.
—Romans 12:2 NIV

Attitude plays a major role in determining what we achieve in our lifetime. I believe there is a strong correlation between attitude and success. Our attitude determines not only how we view challenges, but also how we respond to them. It is one of our greatest assets and must be protected at all times. Especially in times of adversity. Attitude is an everyday choice. When we wake up, we have a decision to make. We can choose to be positive and upbeat, or pessimistic and somber.

Experience has taught me that life is 20 percent what happens to us and 80 percent how we respond. Attitude will determine whether we overcome or succumb to challenges. Attitude will define the height of our success or the depth of our failure. It will either inspire others or discourage them. It will also attract or repel financial resources. In summation, our attitude will determine our altitude.

During his time in slavery, Joseph had to make a choice every day when he woke up. Was he going to look forward to the new challenges of the day or lament about his lost freedom? Despite his situation, the Bible lets us know he was very successful. It never mentions his anger or disappointment with his circumstances. Somehow, he overcame anger and the hurt he had toward his brothers to be successful. He overcame disappointment and bitterness with Potiphar's wife to excel in Pharaoh's jail. Despite his struggles and setbacks, Joseph was able to maintain an optimistic attitude. Joseph was not ruled by his emotions; rather, he ruled them. The following quote helped to put this in the proper perspective for me: "Gratitude and complaining cannot coexist simultaneously. Choose the one that best serves you" (Hal Elrod).

Protecting our attitude requires bringing the flesh under the control of our spirit man. To do this, we crucify our flesh (body, soul, will, passions, emotions, desires) daily. This means we do not give in to our fleshly desires, but we walk under the guidance of the Holy Spirit. The Bible says that *the person without the Spirit does not accept the things that come from the Spirit of God, but considers them foolishness and cannot understand them, because discerned only through the Spirit* (1 Corinthians 2:14 NIV).

We have to bring every thought into the captivity of Christ. We must resist the Enemy every time he plants a thought that causes us to have doubt or to lose faith. We must be very careful whom we allow to speak into our lives. Prioritizing people who confirm and undergird what God has spoken over us will ensure that negative comments are left standing outside of our view.

When we give diligence to cultivating a positive attitude, we can maintain a laser focus while walking through the preparation season. Controlling our emotions minimizes self-induced detours and delays. We must stop blaming the Enemy for things not happening. Instead, we need to focus our thinking on positive things and cultivate a spirit of gratitude. This is one concept the world has embraced and championed. There are tons of motivational speakers who teach on this subject. Here is a quote I found that summarizes this point. Pay attention to the last sentence:

> *Positive thinking is how you think about the problem. Enthusiasm is how you feel about the problem. The two together determine what you do about the problem.*
> —Norman Vincent Peale

Fear Stops Movement

It's high noon on the grasslands of an African savanna. Herds of antelope and zebras are leisurely grazing on the long grass. The warm breeze carries the sound of chirping birds and monkeys playing in the trees. Suddenly, the roar of a lion shatters the peaceful tranquility. Immediately, every animal freezes in place, paralyzed by fear. Ears listen for the location of the danger. Tension fills the atmosphere while thousands of eyes search frantically for the hunter.

Suddenly, the blur of rushing lions causes the animals to scatter in all directions. After a few minutes of panic, calm descends on the plains. The lions congregate around their latest victory. By invoking fear in the grazing herds, the lions were able to gain an advantage over their faster prey.

It's interesting that the Bible refers to Satan as a roaring lion whose goal is to kill, steal, and destroy. He understands the power of fear and desires to inject it into the heart of every believer to get us to abort our assignment. Fear is the most devastating of all human emotions. "Man has no trouble like the paralyzing effects of fear" (Paul Parker).

Fear is the first response believers experience after the revelation of our future. Its job is to challenge anything that would motivate us to leave the familiar place. Just like the ten Hebrew spies in the book of Numbers, fear will paint a negative picture of the promised land. It will exaggerate the risks and make the obstacles seem insurmountable. It will minimize our abilities and strengths, because it wants us to be afraid of uncertainty associated with the unfamiliar place. The Enemy deploys fear to distract people from walking on God's path of life.

Ever wonder why fear shows up when you want to make a faith move? This is no coincidence. The Enemy has strategically injected fear into your thoughts just like the lions roared to freeze the prey. Unfortunately, fear has stopped many believers from reaching their destiny.

Fear will cause us to be disobedient to God's instructions. It whispers that we are not good enough or smart enough. It tells us we are not worthy. Fear causes us to only see why we *shouldn't* instead of why we *should*. It spawns delays and procrastination. It can cause us to abort walking into our promised land because of negative self-perceptions. It will cause us to view our threats and challenges as being larger than our God. That's right. If we are saying we can't when God says we can, we are committing idolatry. In that instant, we have made our problem bigger and stronger than our God.

Forgive us, Lord, for making an idol of our fears.

James F. Bell says, "Fear is an insidious virus. Given a breeding place in our minds ... it will eat away our spirit and block the forward path of our endeavors."

Fortunately, we know that fear is not of God. The Bible says, *God hath not given us the spirit of fear, but of power, and of love and of a sound mind* (2 Timothy 1:7 KJV). The antidote for fear is faith. It is the unshakeable belief that no problem is bigger than God. It's knowing that God enables the called and His strength is made perfect in our weakness. Simply put, if we can trust Him and be obedient, He promises to guide our steps and lead us down the path to our destiny.

So where are you today? Has fear caused you to stop moving? Or, are you walking by faith and leaving your fears behind?

As a rule, the things we fear are not as overwhelming as we think. There is a popular acronym for fear which I have heard used in church. "FEAR is False Evidence Appearing Real." Whenever I push past my fears, I realize the thing I feared was not as bad as I thought it would be. In my mind, I had blown the thing way out of proportion.

The Bible is full of people who had to face their fears on the path to their destiny. David faced his Goliath. Moses faced his audience. Rehab faced her past. And Peter faced his unbelief. All were successful in achieving their destinies, and so will you. Author John Ortberg summed it up best in the title of his book *If You Want to Walk on Water, You've Got to Get out of the Boat.*

Calling all water-walkers. The overflow blessing is waiting for you. Here is another good quote to ponder: "The way to see Faith is to shut the eye of Reason" (Benjamin Franklin).

For me, I had to learn to walk afraid, which reminds me of the time I spoke to the congregation about our capital campaign. I had been in prayer all week about what to say and which Scripture to use. Sunday morning arrived, and I had not received any revelation. As I drove to church, I had to combat the rising fear by speaking Scriptures over my circumstances.

Just before my part in the service, I slowly walked up on the platform and nervously awaited my turn to speak. When I looked out on the faces of the congregation, fear crept into my spirit again. I remember praying, *Lord, You have to give me something to say.*

Thirty seconds before I was to speak, He gave me a Scripture. When I read it, I knew exactly what to say. Afterward, I received many compliments about the passion and clarity of my message. I laughed at the comments, because I knew what they heard was not me, but God speaking through me. That experience taught me to walk and let my faith catch up with me.

If you are struggling with fear, I want you to do four things daily to strengthen your faith. When these steps become your new habit, you will see the power of fear broken from your life. Don't get me wrong, you will continue experiencing fear, because it is a natural response. But you will not allow it to stop you from walking in your daily assignments.

- Speak God's promises for your life.
- Challenge negative thoughts with the Word of God.
- Speak positive affirmations over your life.
- Allow God to fight your battles.

Depression Kills Hope

One of the biggest challenges believers face during the preparation process is allowing our will to die in order to align with God's plan for our lives. During this time, we are constantly warring with our flesh. This is the time when the spirit of depression can sneak in and overcome believers. This spirit attacks our hope in order to weaken our faith, undermine our resolve, and drain our energy.

To combat this spirit, we must be disciplined in spending time in God's presence daily. This simple step can determine whether or not we walk in victory during the preparation season. I have learned that depression and sadness cannot exist in God's marvelous presence. The light of His glory will repel the darkness that seeks to strangle our faith. Those who can encounter God's presence on a daily basis will experience a renewal of their hope and a refreshing of their spirit. This will enable us to endure the preparation season with joy and peace.

How do we experience God's divine presence? Simply by worshipping and praising Him with the fruit of our lips. The Bible says God inhabits the praises of His people (Psalm 22:3). The next time you sense the darkness, put on your favorite worship music and sing until His glory fills your soul with peace and joy.

Keep Your Eyes on the Prize

While we are in the preparation process, emotions can cause us to lose sight of our vision. They will want to revolt against being obedient during the season of trials and testing and verbally assault the people God uses to test and perfect our character. Emotions will desire to express dissatisfaction with where we are and lament on what we had. They will cause us to negatively react to people who are not going where we are going. We will also question our sanity along the journey. Our emotions cannot see the final destination. They can only respond to stimuli along the journey. It is our faith that can see the vision and God's hand at work in our lives. We must keep our eyes on the prize of the overflow blessing.

When Franklin Roosevelt was elected President in 1932, he faced daunting challenges. The nation was in the midst of the Great Depression. Millions of people were out of work, and 11,000 out of 22,000 banks had failed, destroying the savings of depositors. Naturally, Roosevelt's immediate concern was reviving the American economy and getting people back to work. In his inauguration speech, he spoke to a nation that was afraid and disillusioned. He began his speech by addressing the one thing that threatened the psyche of the nation.

> *So, first of all, let me assert my firm belief that the only thing we have to fear is fear itself—nameless, unreasoning, unjustified terror which paralyzes needed efforts to convert retreat into advance. In every dark hour of our national life, a leadership of frankness and of vigor has met with that understanding and support of the people themselves which is essential to victory. And I am convinced that you will again give that support to leadership in these critical days.*
>
> —Franklin D. Roosevelt

Roosevelt knew the importance of keeping our eye on the prize.

His administration embarked on a series of drastic actions that put people to work and gave them hope. To give people something to focus on, they launched a war against the Great Depression. Unlike any of his predecessors, Roosevelt used unprecedented executive powers (typically only granted during wartime) to expand the government and the services it provided. Under his leadership, the nation shifted their focus from existing economic hardships to the new government programs that offered jobs and hope. In time, Roosevelt's "New Deal" policies put the nation on the path to economic recovery.

The Enemy understands the significance of keeping our eye on the prize. That's why he is going to do everything he can to obscure our vision so we lose sight of the prize. To achieve this, he will parade distractions and counterfeits across our line of sight to distract us. These things will seem good, and they will address immediate concerns or needs. But they are not the great thing God has for us. The Enemy hopes to entice our flesh so we will settle for less than what God wants us to have. This is why it is so important to have vision. It serves as a constant reminder of the *excellent* thing God wants for us. Hopefully, this will keep us from falling prey to the Enemy's distractions and counterfeits.

Whatever you look at, you move toward. What are you looking at today? Your past or your future?

Here is a simple tip to keep your eye on the prize. Years ago, my pastor encouraged the congregation to develop a vision board. He instructed us to place it in a prominent place in our homes where we would see it every day. He was teaching us to always keep the prize in our mind—*and sight*. That way, we can evaluate every situation or opportunity by whether it advances us to the vision or takes us away from it. Remember, the vision points to our destination. It allows us to live life on purpose daily.

Don't grow weary in running your race. You will reap a reward when you reach your destination. The overflow blessing is waiting for you.

Addressing that Critical Spirit

A critical spirit wars against our faith, because it longs to be in total control of everything. An individual with this spirit will resist the situations designed to prepare them to be blessed. They will rationalize every reason why they can't obtain what God has for them.

This is a word of caution to those who have a critical spirit.

In case you're wondering if you're part of the crowd, consider these characteristics. Those with such a spirit are quick to judge a work in progress. They will demand perfection at the expense of progress and refuse to move until everything is just right. This person will experience difficulties during the preparation process because they struggle to adapt to change. For them, the unfamiliar place represents a thousand questions with no answers. They will resist the process God has ordained to prepare them for the next level. The good news is God can achieve His perfect will using imperfect vessels.

Let me share how God dealt with me on this subject. As a youth, I developed a critical spirit that excelled at finding fault in everything. Later, the Myers-Briggs personality assessment tool classified me as an ISTJ (introvert, sensing, thinking, judging person). That means I tend to be logical, factual, analytical, responsible, conservative, decisive, consistent, and responsible.

I am also very critical in my analysis of situations. For some unknown reason, I equated excellence with perfection. Instead of pointing out the nine things that were done well, I would point out the one thing that was below expectations. Even in my performance reviews, I was more comfortable listening to my developmental needs rather than my strengths and accomplishments. That mindset created an internal struggle, because I could never live up to my own expectations.

My personality type caused problems when I was hired to get a struggling manufacturing operations group back on its feet. At that time, the culture in the plant was in limbo since the self-directed workforce program had been suspended. The workforce was accustomed to having input on every decision made in the plant. When I came on board, all of that changed.

Being an outsider, I immediately saw everything wrong with the culture and began to change things to address discipline and accountability issues. Although we experienced significant improvements in a short amount of time, I developed a reputation of not caring about people. This was far from the truth. Fortunately, the senior leadership team understood this, so they hired a life coach to work with me.

After our first meeting, the coach gave me an assignment to write down five things I was grateful for daily for thirty days. Initially, this proved to be very difficult, because I struggled to find things to be grateful for. Some days I only came up with two or three things. Wow, that sounds crazy to me now. Thank God for changing me.

Back to the story. Near the end of the thirty days, something happened. I started seeing more of the good things that surrounded me every day. At that moment, I experienced a major inflection point in my life. The realization that I was complaining about the 5 percent instead of enjoying the 95 percent of life caused me to change my mindset.

That exercise taught me to see the world from the glass half full lens. Slowly, my critical eye gave way to an appreciating eye. Instead of immediately looking for what was wrong, I learned to look at what was right. Now, I seek to only speak about the good things that can be found in every person and situation. Now, when I look at people, I realize I am looking at God's creation. My prayer is that I see them through His lens. This balanced perspective helped me to become a better person, friend, and leader. It also stopped me from sabotaging God's plans for my life.

If you are struggling in this area, ask God to show you how He made the people you are critical of. It will totally change your perspective.

The Power of Forgiveness

Unforgiveness chains us to the past, which prevents us from fulfilling our destiny. It opens the door for anger, jealousy, and envy to distract and derail us from the process God is taking us through. When we are in the season of preparation, many things will happen that will require us to forgive in order to stay on the path. Failing to forgive provides the Enemy with an open door to inflame our emotions and distract us off the path to our destiny.

Imagine if Joseph had not forgiven his brothers before they were reunited. The course of history could have been altered if Joseph chose a path of revenge. Without the nation of Israel, there would not be a bloodline for Jesus to enter the world, and Satan could claim victory. Fortunately, God had other plans.

Jesus fulfilled His earthly assignment when He died on the cross for the sins of the world. After His last breath, the veil separating man from God was torn. Instead of bringing judgment and damnation, Jesus brought reconciliation and hope. The power of forgiveness was released into the earth.

To forgive means to stop feeling angry or resentful toward (someone) for an offense, flaw, or mistake, or to cancel a debt. Our sins represent our past mistakes, errors in judgment, or fleshly desires. When we repent and apply the blood of Jesus to wash us clean, God removes our transgression from us as far as the east is from the west (Psalm 103:12). Forgiveness is the key to breaking the chains of the past.

Sadly, many believers are running the Christian race with the weight of the past hanging around their neck. This weight comes from emotional wounds of the past that have not been forgiven. When we don't forgive promptly, these wounds become emotional baggage that we carry around on our journey. Over time, the bag becomes so big it can block out our destiny, drain our willpower, and cause us to drop out of the race.

Imagine trying to compete in a race with a twenty-pound weight on your back. Fortunately, forgiveness allows us to heal emotional wounds and empty the baggage. When we practice forgiveness, we stop carrying unnecessary weight that hinders our ability to complete the race. Unencumbered by the weight, we can run faster and farther with more energy.

I remember the weight that lifted off me when I forgave my mother shortly before she died. Not long after I lost my job in 2012, my mother had emergency surgery for intestinal bleeding. After spending several weeks in a rehabilitation center, I realized she could no longer live by herself. I moved her into my house only to experience an epic clash of personalities during the first week. In my prayer time, I inquired about the source of our poor interaction. The Lord revealed that I possessed unforgiveness in my heart toward her. Once I forgave her, there was a remarkable change in my behavior. Slowly, her behavior changed as well, and a wonderful peace resulted.

Little did I know God was redeeming our relationship. During the last eighteen months of her life, we talked and laughed more than ever. The love between a son and a mother was restored. Looking back, I am grateful God allowed me to heal while she was alive. I only have positive memories and no regrets. And it all started with the simple act of forgiveness.

Years later, I heard Pastor Van Moody say "forgiveness is the key to one person feeling better and another person feeling bitter." Forgiveness allows us to let go of past hurts and pains to live and prosper in the now. The Enemy loves to bring up past hurts and pains to distract us from walking out our destiny.

How many of you know how difficult it is to drive a car when you are always looking in the rearview mirror? I worry that some of you reading this book have pulled off the road to stare at the past through a constant stream of tears. You have spent so much time dealing with frustration, pain, and anguish that you are now bitter and resentful. Unfortunately, this has caused you to stop moving forward. But today, I challenge you to shift the object of your focus from the pain of the past to the God of your future. Seek His guidance to get you back on the path leading to your destiny. All is not lost. God allows U-turns.

Televangelist Joyce Myers once said that "unforgiveness is like drinking poison and expecting the other person to die." Many people are slowly dying while they are waiting for bad things to happen to those who hurt them. Because they are chained to their past, they live unfulfilled lives, because they did not achieve their destiny.

Joseph found a way to not only forgive his brothers but to embrace them with love. Most people would never speak to their brothers if they sold them into slavery. But Joseph knew everything happened according to God's plan for his life.

The same holds true for you today. Don't allow unforgiveness to stop you from moving toward your destiny. There are people who are depending on you to fulfill your purpose.

When Jacob learned there was grain in Egypt, he sent ten of his sons to purchase some. When they arrived, the brothers did not recognize the man selling grain was Joseph. But Joseph recognized them, and through carefully orchestrated events, he was able to reunite the family. When he could no longer contain his joy at seeing his brothers again, Joseph revealed his identity.

Then Joseph said to his brothers, "Come close to me." When they had done so, he said, "I am your brother Joseph, the one you sold into Egypt! And now, do not be distressed and do not be angry with yourselves for selling me here, because it was to save lives that God sent me ahead of you. For two years now there has been famine in the land, and for the next five years there will not be plowing and reaping. But God sent me ahead of you to preserve for you a remnant on earth and to save your lives by a great deliverance."

—Genesis 45:4-7 NIV

During the process of enduring hardships, setbacks, and

disappointments, Joseph experienced the power of forgiveness. When he finally came into a position of power, he did not retaliate against those who had wronged him. He realized God had allowed everything to happen so that one day he would be able to save his family. In Genesis 50:20 Joseph tells his brothers, *You intended to harm me, but God intended it for good to accomplish what is now being done, the saving of many lives* (NIV).

Instead of paying back the evil deed of his brothers, Joseph chose to embrace them with love, thereby fulfilling his destiny. Ultimately, Joseph blessed the family by giving them the fertile plains of Goshen. There, the descendants of all Jacob's sons prospered and multiplied. Because of Joseph's simple act of forgiveness, the twelve tribes of Israel came into existence.

Don't let unforgiveness detour you from the path to your destiny. Who do you need to forgive?

Summary

Emotions are a natural response to external and internal stimuli. They convey our feelings at any point in time. They directly influence our thinking and actions. It is imperative that we learn to manage our emotions and not allow them to drive us.

Destiny achievers have learned the importance of managing their emotions along the journey. This means not getting too high when things go well and not digging a coal mine when things do not go as expected. They resist allowing their emotions to blind them from achieving their destiny.

Despite how he felt, Joseph knew he was called to something higher than being a slave in Potiphar's house. Joseph was focused on making the best of each day. Abraham Lincoln's focus was on healing the nation instead of punishing the vanquished. Franklin Roosevelt encouraged the nation to look past its fears to rebuild a positive economic landscape.

You must do the same. Achieving your destiny will require overcoming your emotions. Let this be the day you stop allowing your emotions to control your life.

No longer will you allow fear to stop you from progressing toward the things of God. When the Enemy sows seeds of doubt and fear, you will immediately speak Scriptures that cause the Enemy to flee. Your daily confessions of faith will enable you to thrive in the now while walking toward your destiny. Your past becomes a place to visit but not to stay. Forgiveness has broken the chains that bound you to the past. No longer do you camp out for a season in the past instead of living for today. That critical spirit has been replaced by a spirit of gratitude, which allows you to see the good in every situation.

Now, you rejoice in the trials and tests you face, because you know they are preparing you for something greater. Your perspective on life speaks to better days ahead of you instead of behind you. Thoughts of your future bring rays of hope on the most challenging days.

Finally, your positive attitude continually thwarts the Enemy's attempts to sidetrack you using your emotions. With these newfound abilities, you can effectively navigate the path toward your destiny.

Reflection Questions:

1. What does God's Word say about your obstacle?

2. What problems are you making larger than your God?

3. If your friends were to describe your attitude during this season, what would they say?

4. Describe the process you use daily to keep your eyes on the prize.

5. Is there an area where unforgiveness is holding you back from God's plan? If so, what steps are you taking to address this?

Meditation Scriptures:

Philippians 3:14
Colossians 3:13
Ephesians 4:31-32
Galatians 6:9-10

CHAPTER EIGHT

Divine Elevation and Promotion

For promotion cometh neither from the east, nor from the west, nor from the south. But God is the judge; He putteth down one and setteth up another.

—Psalm 75:6-7 KJV

AMERICANS LOVE RAGS-TO-RICHES stories. Right now, someone is dreaming about hitting the jackpot and winning a lot of money. They long for a blessing that will sustain them and have them lacking for nothing. But instead of turning to God, many people will seek out the devices of man to find their fortune.

Some look for a quick return by playing the sweepstakes, Powerball, and other get-rich-quick games. Others take a longer approach to wealth. This may involve sacrificing a portion of their wages and making smart investments in real estate and the stock market. Musicians and singers dream about writing the hit song that will propel them to infamy. Salesmen fantasize about winning the big order. Writers long to write a national best-seller. All hope for one thing: to be able to live a better life.

Mature believers understand that God is our source, and He will provide all our needs. The church has been brainwashed to think piety and poverty are synonymous. This is far from the truth. When we study Joseph's promotion, Solomon's wealth, David's kingship, or the apostle Paul's wisdom, we find that God was the source. He elevated them and provided the knowledge they needed to prosper on the earth. The Lord desires to bless His people so we can be a blessing to others. Out of our overflow, believers will be able to give joyfully.

Divine elevation and promotion require aligning with God's will for our lives. In the previous chapters, we discussed God's transformation process. As we submit to His will and obey His precepts, we can walk the path He has illuminated for us. For those who complete the journey, we are ready to walk in the next level of blessing. Sadly, some people forsake their blessing because they don't want to leave the familiar place. Others give up in the wilderness season because they are unable to grow and change. For those who endure, the transformation process has prepared them to walk into the fullness of their destiny.

God's Plan for Promotion

When it comes to promotion and elevation, God looks at things differently than the world. The world touts the capability of the individual, whereas God looks at the heart of the person. When we look at successful people in the Bible, they all exhibited similar characteristics. They were faithful in their actions, obedient to the guidance of God, and humble in their faith-walk. They operated in His divine favor and were subsequently elevated at the appointed time.

People such as Enoch, Abraham, Moses, Joshua, Gideon, Deborah, Elisha, David, and Paul experienced divine elevation and promotion. They understood the importance of completing their assignments and relying totally on God for guidance. They subjected their carnality under the control of their spirit man to fulfill their destiny. Studying their stories provided me with key insights on trusting the Lord's promotion process.

When God elevates people, it is not based on what they have earned or accomplished. He is concerned about the condition of the heart. Proverbs 23:7 says *as a man thinketh in his heart, so is he* (KJV).

Before we enter the transformation process, our hearts are focused solely on the desires of the flesh. When we exit the transformation process, our hearts are focused on pleasing God by doing his will. God desires our hearts to be focused solely on Him. He desires us to fellowship with Him throughout each day for everything we need. When our hears are fully transformed, He can trust us to do His divine will.

Faithfulness and obedience work to keep us in a place where God can transform our heart. They enable us to progress through the wilderness period in order for the transformation process to complete its perfect work. When the transformation is complete, people will not see the individual. They will see God in the individual. That is, people will see how our character reflects the character of our Lord and Savior.

When people look at you, what do they see?

Based on what you have read so far, are you ready to receive your blessing? This is a sticky question for a lot of people. Many are quick to look at their accomplishments and assume they are ready for the next level. They have punched all the prerequisite tickets such as completing training classes and assignments, been recognized for certain accomplishments, and so on. The trouble is, they have neglected growing their character, which reflects the condition of the heart.

I was one of those people who was driven by outward accomplishments rather than inward growth. While I achieved a certain level of success operating in my own flesh, I came nowhere close to achieving the overflow blessing, which requires much more than mere human effort to be good.

My perspective on elevation changed when I was in the midst of a long wilderness season. In retrospect, each setback and disappointment served to tenderize my heart so the Word of God could take root. I found myself studying and memorizing Scriptures to get me through challenging weeks. Slowly, my will began to die, and His will became the desire of my heart. Next, He showed me how to see people in a different light. Instead of seeing their failures and shortcomings, I saw their abilities and potential. Over time, I learned to look past their pain and emotional scars to see them the way God created them. As that critical spirit died in me, it was replaced with compassion and love.

Looking back, I realize now that God was renovating my heart to reflect His heart for mankind. In my darkest days, God nurtured a new light inside of me that ultimately transformed my life. My character changed for the better. Then He opened the door for me to walk into my destiny. I'm assured He will do the same thing for you. Just like Moses, God is equipping you to move to a higher level. Just remember that God equips those He calls to do great things. Be encouraged. You are closer to your blessing than you think. The question is will you wait on God to elevate you?

Stop Worrying About Closed Doors

God's plan to elevate Joseph involved closing doors to the past before opening doors to the future. On that fateful day his angry brothers sold Joseph into slavery, it pushed him on the path toward his destiny. The painful truth is that God's plan for your life will require some doors to be closed. Stop worrying and complaining about closed doors that are not tied to your destiny. Trust that God has something bigger and better in store for you. When you complete the transformation process, your latter days will be greater.

The Enemy is watching how we respond to a closed door. He desires to distract us by making us dwell on the lost opportunity. He reminds us of the good things we had, causing us to long for the past. He will pull on our emotions to get us to grieve about lost opportunities instead of focusing on the future. Hopefully, mature believers will recognize this subtle attack and reject it immediately, because they have learned to rejoice when God allows a door to close. That is a signal a new door is about to open soon.

For many of you, the path to the overflow blessing will involve several doors closing before you walk into your destiny. Some of you may be asking why God closed certain doors. The blunt answer is that many of us needed to be kick-started into our destiny. My opinion is that closed doors will do that quicker than anything else. Let's be honest, the wilderness is not a place many of us want to visit on our own accord. But the Bible tells us *many are the afflictions of the righteous, but the Lord delivereth him out of them all* (Psalm 34:19 KJV).

We have to cross the wilderness in order to receive what God has for us. Instead of complaining like the freed Hebrew slaves, now is the time to put faith in motion and endure the transformation process.

The good news is when God closes one door, He will open another one for those who are obedient to His will. And there is nothing the Enemy can do to stop God. When God closed the door on Joseph's life as a herdsman, He opened the door for him to lead Potiphar's house. At the right time, God closed the door at Potiphar's house, which positioned Joseph to meet Pharaoh's officials in prison. At the right time, God reminded the official of Joseph. This opened the door for Joseph to meet Pharaoh and solve his problems.

Don't despair over closed doors and missed opportunities. In due season, God will open a new door that will supersede anything you can dream or imagine. The challenge is being diligent in the now to prepare for that wonderful day.

The timing for the opening will depend upon our ability to navigate through the transformation process. How long will it take for us to learn how to manage our emotions while walking by faith? How long will it take for us to learn how to crucify our flesh in order to do His will? How long will it take for our selfish heart to be transformed into His selfless love? That's how long it will take for the door to the overflow blessing to be opened.

Regardless of the doors that have been closed in your life, trust and believe that God will open another door which leads to greater things. Your latter days will be greater than your former days. To dispel any doubt, this is your Father's guarantee: *Forget the former things; do not dwell on the past. See, I am doing a new thing! Now it springs up; do you not perceive it?* (Isaiah 43:18-19 NIV).

God Promotes the Humble

Previously, we discussed how God looks for someone to promote. He examines the heart of the individual. He looks for selfless individuals who are totally dependent on Him. God desires to elevate humble people who have prepared themselves to receive—those who trust Him explicitly and in whom He trusts.

- Those who have been found faithful and obedient to His voice.

- Those who no longer allow emotions or desires to override their spirit man.

- Those who are committed to God having the final say in their lives.

- Those who are dependent on God for both guidance and provision.

- Those who have lost faith in their flesh and have great faith in the God they serve. He wants to position them in key places in the marketplace to bear witness for Him.

- Those who have been found worthy will be carriers of God's glory on earth.

God opposes the proud but shows favor to the humble (James 4:6 NIV). How many believers have struggled with this statement?

Especially when we look around and see self-marketing people being promoted every week. You know the ones. They are always networking with the higher-ups. Playing golf after work and socializing with them during the weekends. Isn't that the way to get promoted? What are we supposed to do as believers? Don't get me wrong, networking is very important for building and fostering relationships. But for believers, we must understand that God defines our future.

We serve a sovereign God whose methods are different from those of the world. Frankly, He is looking to promote those who trust Him. Not the arrogant, conceited, self-centered person who pulled himself up by the boot straps. Ouch, that statement still hurts me. *For those who exalt themselves will be humbled, and those who humble themselves will be exalted* (Matthew 23:12 NIV).

The world would have us believe humility is synonymous with weakness. That is a lie of the Enemy. It takes strength to love those who hate you. It takes courage and fortitude to turn the other check and be quick to forgive. Let's set the record straight (and our thinking) by looking at the definition of the word.

Humility means to have a modest opinion of one's own importance. It is a quality of being courteously respectful of others. Humility fosters peace and harmony by affirming the value of others over self. Humility is the opposite of pride. Pride emphasizes the importance of self. This is in contrast to humility, which emphasizes the importance of others. If you are always busy supporting and promoting others, who is doing that for you? The answer can be found in James 4:10: *Humble yourselves before the Lord, and he will lift you up* (NIV).

When the world looks at humble people, they see past the flesh to see the God of the individual. The actions of humble believers reflect the fruit of the Spirit, and their wisdom and insight surpass that provided by natural senses. But more importantly, they will not steal God's glory. The desire to magnify their flesh has died and been replaced by the desire to glorify God in all they do. They have become skilled at crucifying their desires in order to focus solely on walking in the will of God. Joseph was such an individual. Even pagans recognized God's Spirit moving in his life. The seasons of trials and testing matured Joseph to be a vessel of honor to carry God's glory. *He guides the humble in what is right and teaches them his way* (Psalm 25:9 NIV).

Before we leave this point, let's look at the some of the key traits of humble people. Humble people:

- Endure hardships without complaining.

- Find joy and peace in any environment.

- Sow into the visions of other people.

- Are quick to give credit and to take the blame.

- Seek to affirm others rather than self.

- Celebrate the success of others.

- Seek to learn first. They are teachable.

The absence of humility will disqualify you from receiving the overflow blessing. How did I reach that conclusion? The Bible says God opposes the proud (James 4:6) and He exalts the humble (Matthew 23:12). Don't get mad at me. These are not my words.

Focus on developing a humble spirit. That is what God is looking for.

If you are anxious about God elevating you, I suggest reviewing how you are dealing with pride. Don't allow pride to disqualify you from being elevated. If you are struggling with your pride, pray for grace to accept the perfect will of God. Then apply Romans 8:28 to everything that happens in your lives. Place greater emphasis on your prayer time and your reading time. This is where your heart will be transformed so that love and compassion can overshadow pride.

Pray this prayer: *Thank you, Jesus, for being a marvelous example of walking in humility and power. You showed us what it means to walk humbly before the Lord.*

Your Gifts Solve Problems

The overflow blessing is always tied to a problem. The greater the problem, the larger the blessing for those who can solve it, which is why we believers should never run from difficult problems. We need to exercise our faith and embrace these opportunities. After all, we serve the God of creation. No problem is too hard for Him to solve through us as He did for Joseph.

In Genesis chapter 41, Pharaoh was searching for someone to interpret his two dreams. Upon learning about Joseph, Pharaoh had him brought from the prison. When Joseph interpreted the dreams, Pharaoh was faced with a huge problem. How would the nation position itself to survive the upcoming famine? What needed to be done in the prosperous years to prepare for the lean years?

This massive problem represented a big opportunity for Joseph. Neither Pharaoh nor any of his officials and wise counselors knew what to do. But God positioned and equipped Joseph to provide the answer. The time spent in Potiphar's house and in prison developed his gift of management. Pharaoh's dreams represented a simple management problem for Joseph and his God. Joseph provided Pharaoh with a plan to store the excess grain in the good years for use during the years of famine. After conferring with his officials, Pharaoh agreed with the solution. Now, they needed someone to manage the process.

Open doors are often masked by big problems. What problem has God qualified you to solve?

Pharaoh's next statement opened the door to the overflow blessing for Joseph. Pharaoh recognized that only Joseph could solve the management of collecting and disbursing the grain. Wasting no time, he offered Joseph a role in his kingdom. In a single moment, Joseph was promoted to a position of power, second only to Pharaoh. This story not only defies all logic, it also illustrates the faithfulness of God in remembering Joseph.

Let's fast forward to the 21st century. God desires to do similar things for His chosen people who have been found faithful and obedient. Their assignment is not in the church, it is out in the marketplace. As they go about their daily tasks, God is going to bless them with incredible favor. I prophesy that many places will experience new levels of prosperity when disciples of Christ are elevated into positions of leadership.

The overflow blessing is waiting for you. Are you ready?

For His Glory

Are you struggling with the point of God promoting the humble? This was a stumbling block for me until I received this revelation from the Holy Spirit. When God elevates people, He does it in a manner that always points back to Him. The people He elevates will always credit God with being the force behind their success.

News flash: God is jealous of His glory, and He does not want to share it with anyone. That is why he favors those with humble hearts. When God elevates people, it is designed to reveal His power and majesty.

Looking back on Joseph's story, we can see this point illustrated after he interpreted Pharaoh's dreams. In Genesis 41, Pharaoh asked his officials where they could find a man with the Spirit of God on him. I love this part of the story. The leader of a nation who worshipped many gods, recognized the true and living God operating through Joseph. That is a living testimony.

Pharaoh made this statement in light of the ongoing animosity Egyptians felt toward Hebrews. The Bible says shepherds were detestable to the Egyptians. This made me wonder what Pharaoh saw in Joseph that made him overcome his disdain for Hebrews. Clearly, he saw and felt the presence of God operating in and through Joseph. In that moment, the glory of God must have been so strong on Joseph that Pharaoh did something unheard of in that day. He put a detestable Hebrew in charge of running the country. This individual stood above all the wisest men who could be found in Egypt. Pharaoh gave

Joseph the name *Zaphenath-Paneah,* which means one who discovers hidden things. And this consecrated vessel of God successfully led Egypt through the next fourteen years of feast and famine.

If God were to elevate you right now, would people see His hand at work in your life?

When the world senses the presence of God, they will respond in one of two ways. Whether they are attracted to it or repelled by it will be determined by the condition of their heart. Those whose hearts have not been hardened will be drawn like a moth to a flame. While they may not understand what they are experiencing, they do recognize something is different and special. Just like the throngs of people that followed Jesus, they will be enamored with the different manifestations of power. Their logical minds will seek answers to explain what they have witnessed and experienced.

Pharaoh was attracted to the glory operating in Joseph. He could sense something unnatural about the Hebrew transplant, and he wanted that for his kingdom. Because of Joseph, the kingdom of God was welcomed into a formerly hostile place. The favor of God which rested on Joseph blessed Egypt to not only survive the famine but to emerge prosperous and wealthy.

In these final days, God's plan for reaching the lost will require disciples to exercise their faith outside of the church. He desires to elevate mature believers in their respective workplaces in order to expose people to His amazing grace and love. These will be people who have been transformed by their wilderness experiences into vessels of honor for the Master's use.

The Enemy has influenced social media to bombard people with negative messages, fake news, and angry rhetoric. In response to these negative messages, people are starting to lose hope. Fear has crept in due to the rise in natural catastrophes and violent acts against humanity. In this environment, people long for examples of goodness and love to restore their faith. They don't want to be condemned for their sins, and they don't want to be preached to. All they desire is a ray of hope.

Outside the four walls of the church lies the great market place, where billions of unsaved people exist. This is the great opportunity for the body of Christ to witness to people so they may know about the living God. Before his death in 2014, the prophet Bob Jones shared a vision for a billion people being saved in the greatest harvest of souls ever witnessed.

How is this going to happen when we can't get a million people to come to church? The answer is simple. We have to let our lives witness to them in our everyday interactions. In his book *Anointed for Business*, Ed Silvoso wrote, "The Devil is afraid that Christians will fulfill their divine destiny in the marketplace and bring the kingdom of God to it." When we take our rightful place in the marketplace and humbly operate in the love of Christ, we can touch a group of people who have no desire to come to a church.

Imagine the impact we can have in this world. When people can experience the love of God in their jobs, in the stores where they shop, in their schools, and in their communities, He will draw them. All we have to do is be on our post with our transformed lives. Can people see the Lord in the manner that you live your life daily? Jesus said, *No one can come to me unless the Father who sent me draws them, and I will raise them up at the last day* (John 6:44 NIV).

Modern disciples have been called to go forth and be the salt of the earth. Each day we have opportunities to demonstrate the love of Christ with people we interact with. Don't worry, you will not have to pass out tracts and preach. People will pay attention when your behavior reflects peace and love during stressful and chaotic times. When you treat your enemies with love and kindness, they will take note. When you consistently speak positive words over negative situations, it will make them curious. *Who is this person who acts differently than the rest of us?* People will be drawn to you to find out what makes you different. That will be your open door to share the gospel and glorify God.

Are you ready to be a vessel of honor which carries God's glory?

When You Have Done All You Can, Then Rest

I wish I could share when God is going to elevate you, but the reality is no one knows. What I can share is how to make the best use of your time in the meanwhile. For me, waiting was the most difficult part of this process. Imagine how Joseph felt waiting thirteen years or Abraham waiting twenty-five years.

The prophet Isaiah shared some words of wisdom for those whose trust is in the Lord.

He gives strength to the weary and increases the power of the weak. Even youths grow tired and weary, and young men stumble and fall; but those who hope in the Lord will renew their strength. They will soar on wings like eagles; they will run and not grow weary, they will walk and not be faint.
—Isaiah 40:29-31NIV

When you have done all you can, then rest in the knowledge that at the right time God will open the next door. In a previous chapter, we learned God's timing is perfect. What makes waiting on God's timing so difficult? The simple answer is we are focused on the wrong things. Instead of focusing on God, we spend time worrying about when things will happen. This causes us to stop moving and relinquish our peace and joy. Looking back on my wilderness experiences, I allowed my frustration level to peak because of worrying about when the next door would open.

The key to resting in His peace is to shift our focus from worry about what has yet to happen to living in the now of today. It is so easy to lose sight of what we have when we focus on what we don't have. I had friends who continually reminded me about the favor I walked in daily. Even though I had not worked in several years, I had money in the bank, all the bills were paid, and I never lacked for anything. My breakthrough came when I asked the Lord, "What do you want me to do while I wait on you to open the next door?" His answer was simple: *My will for that day.* Now, in my daily prayer time, I invite God to reveal my steps for the day. "Who do you want me to encourage today? What do you want me to accomplish today? Where do you want me to go today?"

If you are in a waiting season, this is a good time to focus on your reading and prayer time. Staying in God's Word will refresh your spirit, energize your soul, and strengthen your faith. Do not despair—you are exactly where you need to be. Maximize each day while you wait for God to open the next door.

Isolation Before Elevation

The period of time just before elevation is often the most challenging. At this stage of the process, we find ourselves passing the majority of our tests. God's Word is hidden deep in our heart, and we cherish spending time in His presence. In facing numerous challenges, we have developed our skills and abilities. This is the time we have to deal with the last obstacle that will prevent us from carrying the weight of the overflow blessing.

This season is characterized by isolation and faltering dreams. All around you, people are being blessed and walking through open doors. Now is the time to deal with your pride. I believe God uses isolation to address our pride. When we are hidden for a season and there is no one to listen to us boast about our past accomplishments, we find ourselves getting real with God. Joseph found himself in this place for two years prior to his fateful meeting with Pharaoh.

When Pharaoh's chief cup bearer left prison, I imagine Joseph felt good about getting out of jail soon. After all, Joseph asked the official to intercede with Pharaoh to get him released from prison. Surely, the official understood that Joseph had been forcibly carried away from his homeland and wrongly jailed for a crime he did not commit. He expected the God that granted him favor in Potiphar's house would intervene to get him released from prison. But the Bible says the cup bearer forgot about Joseph.

Imagine how dejected Joseph must have felt when days turned into weeks and then into months. *Lord, why did you allow this to happen? Why have you forgotten about me?* Why was this allowed to happen?

There remained a part of Joseph that needed to die before God could elevate him and enable him to save his family. Whether it was unforgiveness toward his brothers—or maybe anger toward Potiphar's wife—something needed to be purged from Joseph. His character was not ready to handle the challenges he was going to face. After all, "the higher the level, the greater the Devil." This statement reflects the different levels of challenges one faces when walking in a higher level of God-ordained authority. Our character must be mature to handle greater challenges while we continue to glorify God with our actions and behaviors. Otherwise, the responsibilities and challenges of the next level will overwhelm us.

Our godly character is shaped in the dark side of the wilderness, the place where we feel separated and isolated from the world. Here, our labor seems in vain, because we see no progress toward our destiny. No matter how much we sow in terms of blessing other people and striving for excellence in our work, God's favor seems to impact everyone else.

During this necessary time of isolation, God allows situations to purge and shape our character. When we enter this season, our focus tends to be on self, in particular our desires, needs, and wants. When we exit this season, our focus is solely on fulfilling God's desires for our lives. Moses spent forty years in the desert exchanging arrogance for humility. This time is extremely challenging, because this is where the last vestige of pride must die. Thankfully, God is faithful, and He elevated Joseph at the appropriate time. Since He is no respecter of persons, He will do the same for you. He has bigger things in store for you.

Summary

Wow, it is so freeing to know that as believers we don't have to promote ourselves. We serve a God who opposes the proud and elevates the humble. Once we allow Him to position and prepare us, He is faithful to elevate us at the right time. There is no need to worry and fret over closed doors. We should refrain from being anxious to open new doors. Instead, we can focus on executing God's daily assignment for our lives.

We know that the testing of our faith develops patience, refines our character, and creates humility. The latter is the characteristic God is looking for when He wants to elevate us to the next level. Joseph endured thirteen years in obscurity before God opened a door for him, which led to his elevation.

While you are waiting on God to elevate you, it is imperative that you meditate on His Word day and night so you will not give in and abort the process. Or worse, try to achieve things without God. Remember, the darkest portion of the night occurs right before the dawn. Do not become discouraged if the attacks and negative thoughts intensify. They are designed to cause you to abort the process and forfeit your blessing. The Enemy understands the positive impact your blessing will have on advancing God's kingdom on earth. He is trying to stop you at all costs. You may cry in the night, but joy comes in the morning (Psalm 30:5). You have come too far to quit. Continue walking faithfully, and allow God's perfect will to be done in His perfect timing. Selah!

Reflection Questions:

1. How do people view your life? How would they describe your impact?

2. What have you learned going through the transformation process?

3. What does Philippians 2:3 mean to you?

4. What does it mean to have a humble spirit?

5. Have you met anyone who carried God's glory? How did you feel being around them?

Meditation Scriptures:

Psalm 33:4
Galatians 6:22
James 3:13
James 4:6
Proverbs 22:4
Isaiah 55:

CHAPTER NINE

Redemption and Restoration

Your beginnings will seem humble, so prosperous will your future be.

—Job 8:7 NIV

WHEN I WAS growing up, I remember older Christians saying, "God is an on-time God. He may not be there when you want Him, but He is always there when you need him." My youthful bravado did not allow me to grasp the significance of their words. But in time, my experiences bore witness to the validity of that statement.

It's funny how life has a way of reminding you of the words spoken by wise counsel. Mature believers know God is faithful, and His promises are yes and amen. We have also learned that God's timing seldom correlates with our timing. The challenge is in managing our flesh while we wait on God to move.

I am sure there were many days when Joseph wondered why things were taking so long. Yet he managed to persevere by keeping his focus on God. Isaiah 40:31 says that *those who hope in the Lord will renew their strength* (NIV). If you are anxious for a breakthrough, remember to keep your eyes on the Lord. At the right time, He will open the door to your overflow blessing.

When man looks at progress, he measures it relative to time. By nature, man desires that everything come to fruition in a reasonable amount of time. In other words, we like things to happen quickly. In general, humans do not like to wait for anything. Thanks to recent advances in technology, our expectation for immediate action/ response has significantly increased. Instead of developing long suffering (which equates to patience), we have become the microwave generation. We want everything now. But how many know that man's perspective of time is much different than God's?

The ancient Greeks understood this, because they had two words for time: *Chronos and Kairos*. Chronos refers to sequential time, which is measured and is quantitative. Its opposite, Kairos, is qualitative. It has no beginning and end. It speaks to the right moment, the perfect time. Humans operate in Chronos time, but God operates in Kairos time, which may explain why many of us complain about God taking too long to move on our behalf. But how many know we serve a right-on-time God? He may not move when we want Him to, but He always delivers when we need Him. Ecclesiastes 3:1 reminds us that everything has a place, time and season. God has a specific time to deliver your overflow blessing.

In the Blink of an Eye

Joseph was thirty-one years old when he was elevated to Pharaoh's second in command. Approximately thirteen years had passed since his brothers sold him into slavery. He went from serving Pharaoh's officials in prison to running the country in a matter of days. He traded his filthy prison garments for handcrafted robes of fine linen and fine jewelry. Instead of walking, Joseph was chauffeured around in a richly adorned chariot that signified his position of power and authority in the land. Instead of serving people in the prison, servants were attending to his every need.

On that momentous Kairos day, Joseph woke up longing for freedom and went to sleep a free and powerful man. What an incredible turnaround. From obscurity to authority in the span of one day. When God moves in Kairos time, things happen quickly. What would normally take years to achieve can be accomplished in a matter of days. You can go from the cellar to the penthouse via the express elevator. Nothing is too hard for the Lord.

When God released the overflow blessing on Joseph, there was no time to prepare for it. Like the parable of the ten virgins, opportunity comes to those who are prepared and ready. In the time between the vision and the manifestation, Joseph utilized every opportunity to develop his management and leadership skills. Seasons of hardship and challenges developed his confidence and molded his character. Joseph learned from his failures and developed the ability to embrace change. More importantly, he learned to trust God for everything. In every situation, Joseph's steps were ordered by the Lord. When the time came for him to lead a nation, Joseph was confident and ready. The Enemy realized the significance of this moment and began to bombard Joseph with seeds of doubt. Imagine what the Enemy was whispering in his ear.

- You have never done this before.
- What makes you think you can do this job?
- You are going to fail and embarrass yourself.
- The Egyptians will never obey you.
- You are not smart enough to do the job.
- You are not good enough.
- You are…

Does this sound familiar? What would you do if Pharaoh offered you the position as second in command? How many of us would shout *yes*? How many would hesitate because of doubt? After all, the opportunity represented a significant increase in responsibility. Out of timidity more than anything else, some of us would have had to pray and fast before responding. A few would have politely declined because of fear and insecurity. Not Joseph. He had learned to hear God clearly in his thirteen years of captivity. More importantly, Joseph quickly silenced the voice of doubt whenever new opportunities presented themselves. He stepped boldly into every new assignment, such as running Potiphar's house. He had never run a country, but he was confident that God could. His faith was not in his flesh but in the God whom he served. How many of us have reached this point in our faith walk?

Modern day believers can learn a lot from Joseph's sudden elevation. When God opens the door for elevation, that is not the time to question if you are ready. That is the time to *leap* by faith. The season of isolation has made your spirit very sensitive to a move of God. You are no longer controlled by the desires of your flesh but by your spirit. This means you will quickly recognize when God opens a door for you. Consequently, you must be ready to move *immediately*.

Joseph was in the right place at the right time. More importantly, he was available. Warning: the right time does not last forever. The door is only open for a brief time before it closes. Those who miss it will have to wait another season before it opens again. Those who have completed the transformation process and conquered their fears will boldly step into the new opportunity.

Again, success comes to those who are prepared. "There are no secrets to success. It is the result of preparation, hard work, and learning from failure" (General Colin Powell).

When Pharaoh gave Joseph his personal signet ring, the transfer of power was complete. From that point forward, all decisions in the land of Egypt were made and approved by Joseph. God redeemed the time Joseph spent managing Potiphar's house and the prison jail. Those experiences prepared him to step into this prominent leadership position. The lives of a nation rested on the decisions of this young ruler. From slavery to running a nation in the same day. Because of Joseph's obedience and faithfulness, God redeemed the time he lost in slavery so much that his latter days were greater than his former.

God wants to do the same for you. Your latter days will be greater than your former.

Released into Your Destiny

In his new position, Joseph took action to prepare the country for the coming famine. He traveled across the land implementing programs to collect and store food near the cities where it was collected. This work required a significant amount of coordination across a multitude of people.

Storage facilities had to be constructed, food collection processes implemented, people hired, and storage management systems developed. Every system was successful, and the favor of God continued to operate in Joseph's life. The years of abundant harvest allowed Egypt to store up massive quantities of grain. During this time, Pharaoh gave Joseph a wife who bore him two sons, Manasseh and Ephraim. Joseph prospered immensely with his new family.

As assured by God, after seven years of abundant harvest, Egypt entered a season of famine. When the crops failed, people cried out to Pharaoh for help. Because of Joseph's sound management skills, there was food in Egypt. His revolutionary programs were ready to save the nation. With famine spreading over the country, Joseph opened the storehouses and sold grain to the Egyptians.

Soon, the famine spread to neighboring countries. As news spread about the availability of grain in Egypt, people traveled from faraway lands to purchase food to survive. Two years into the famine, a Hebrew father decided to send his sons to Egypt to purchase some grain so they would not starve. God was about to redeem the first dream young Joseph shared with his brothers many years before.

When the brothers (minus the youngest, Benjamin) arrived in Egypt, they sought out the governor who oversaw the distribution of grain (Genesis 42). Upon meeting him, they bowed down with their faces on the ground. While they did not recognize Joseph, Joseph recognized them. The first dream of the sheaves bowing down to him was fulfilled. Joseph's response to his brothers was interesting. Instead of revealing himself immediately, he played a game of deception, which some scholars argue was to determine the status of their heart. This resulted in their making two trips to Egypt before Joseph finally revealed that he was their brother. Eventually, he was reunited with his family, and the second dream was fulfilled.

The overflow blessing will restore all that was lost or taken from you while you were going through the transformation process. It is your reward for obediently enduring seasons of trials and testing and being found faithful by the Lord. Because of your perseverance, you will now walk in a season of favor, engulfed by a blessing so big, you forget the pain and anguish you felt when going through the process.

As foretold in Scripture, the promise of God will be fulfilled, because your latter days will be greater than your former days. We can see this principle in action in Joseph's story. Genesis 41, verses 51 and 52 shed some interesting light on how the overflow blessing impacted his life.

> *Joseph named his firstborn Manasseh and said, "It is because God has made me forget all my trouble and all my family's household." The second son he named Ephraim and said "It is because God has made me fruitful in the land of my suffering." (NIV)*

From both verses you can well imagine that Joseph found a wondrous peace in his new life. Let's focus on verse 51. God's blessing made Joseph forget about his troubles and the painful separation from his family. The memories of being sold into slavery, of being imprisoned, and lied about no longer haunted him. Clearly, Joseph did not forget the trauma that happened to him. He was human, not divine. But there was no emotional pain associated with the memories. Why? Because God healed him from that emotional pain.

It is interesting to note that despite his position of power, Joseph made no immediate attempt to re-establish contact with his family. Nor did he leave the land of his suffering. Instead, God transformed the desert of his Egyptian slavery into an oasis of vibrant life for Joseph. His current situation left no room for reflecting on his previous life in Canaan.

The same will happen to you. God will redeem you where you are. Your place of suffering will transform into a place of prosperity. Things will happen rapidly in this new season. Let us take a lesson from Joseph and not dwell on the former things. Our focus should be on the new thing God is doing. *I will restore to you the years that the locust hath eaten, the cankerworm, and the caterpillar, and the palmerworm, my great army which I sent among you* (Joel 2:25 KJV).

It was God's Plan

Mighty men and women of the Bible often failed to sense the greatness inside of them. Moses, who stuttered, didn't want to talk to Pharaoh. Gideon, who was the weakest in his clan, scoffed at being a warrior. Esther did not want to go before the king. Jonah rebelled and tried to flee from his Nineveh assignment. Saul, who struggled with personal insecurities, did not want to be king. David had problems with controlling his flesh. But these ordinary individuals with their weaknesses went on to do extraordinary things, because God had a plan for them. Regardless of their flaws or how they felt, God used them to achieve His will on earth. And He has a plan for your life. Remember Romans 8:28: *In all things God works for the good of those who love Him, who have been called according to His purpose* (NIV).

Joseph understood this principle when he finally revealed himself in Genesis 45:1-8 to his brothers. He acknowledged that everything happened according to God's will for his life. He told them not to be angry with themselves for selling him, because it was part of God's plan—for the salvation of Israel.

> *But God sent me ahead of you to preserve for you a remnant on earth and to save your lives by a great deliverance. So then, it was not you who sent me here, but God.*
> —Genesis 45:7-8 NIV

This statement reveals a lot about Joseph's heart. Over twenty years had passed since that terrible day. With malice toward none, Joseph attributed their cruel act to divine providence. Instead of blaming his brothers, he stated that God orchestrated the events. Joseph saw how God allowed things to happen to ensure he would end up in Egypt. Fortunately for his brothers, Joseph's years of sacrifices ultimately positioned him to save a nation and bless their family. God had a plan. By faith, Joseph trusted the Lord to deliver and sustain him.

Looking back over your past, can you see the hand of God moving in your life? The traps He spared you from? The grace that covered your errors? The accidents He saved you from? The favor you walked in? Just like Joseph, God has a plan for your life. Maybe it's time to abandon your personal plans and allow God to establish them. Proverbs 16:3 says, *Commit to the Lord whatever you do, and He will establish your plans* (NIV).

God often uses individuals and circumstances to agitate His people into leaving the comfortable place. Unfortunately, some of us spend too much time focusing on the wrong that was perpetrated against us instead of where God wants us to go next. Joseph's response to his brothers offers believers a powerful teaching point. I believe we should mimic Joseph's humility and gratitude when facing the equivalent of his brothers and their cruelty. In retrospect, his brothers were simply operating in God's plan.

When we look at our circumstances, maybe God is allowing events and people to push us into our destiny. The painful truth is they are not trying to hurt you; they are being prompted by God so His will can be carried out.

Televangelist Joel Olsteen summed it up best when he said, "*This* had to happen for *that* to happen." How many of us can embrace and accept that statement? Let's face it, Joseph would not have ventured to Egypt on his own accord. During that time, Egyptians viewed Hebrews as inferior people and chose not to associate with them. To get him there at all, it was crucial for his brothers to abduct him and sell him into slavery.

Think about your current situation. I suspect God allowed a door to close that you would not have closed on your own. For me, it involved losing a job where I had enjoyed years of supernatural favor.

It was early spring in 2012 when I was channel surfing on TV and came across Joel Olsteen preaching about God opening and closing doors. When he made the statement I mentioned above, the wounds from losing my job were still fresh. I struggled with feelings of anger and betrayal. *Why did this happen to me?*

When I heard Joel make that statement, it resonated within me that I *had* to lose my job. I wrote down his words on a piece of paper and taped it on my bathroom mirror. Every day, I would read it aloud to remind myself that God is sovereign in my life, and everything happens for a reason.

Don't get me wrong, there were days when it was difficult to accept this concept. Ultimately, I found great peace. Corporate America was my comfortable place, but God had something bigger in store for me—something that better corresponded with my passion for music and teaching. Over the next several months, God shared a vision with me, and I embarked on creating a business plan. Little did I know this book would be one of the fruits from that time of isolation from family, friends, associates, and others… all because I lost my job. God knew, and at the right time, He redeemed the vision He gave me.

Let there be no doubt, God has a plan for our lives. It is important not to hold a grudge against the people God uses to get us to move toward our blessing. We must forgive and celebrate them, letting grace and mercy govern our thoughts when we think about them. If the wrong they did had not agitated us out of the comfortable place, we would have never reached our destiny. Remember, it only takes a speck of sand to irritate an oyster to produce a beautiful pearl.

Looking back, I can see how God sent agitators to signal my seasons coming to an end. Over time, I have learned to forgive them. Thankfully, God healed my heart and positioned me for the next season of my life.

Who was the agitator in your life? Have you thanked them for getting you out of the comfortable place?

Redemption

Redemption is defined as the action of regaining or gaining possession of something in exchange for payment of; clearing a debt; or the act of paying a ransom to return something to your possession. The Greek word for redemption is *agorazo,* which means "to purchase in the market place." In ancient times, the word was often used in the context of purchasing a slave's freedom.

This concept is best illustrated in the life of Jesus. Jesus left his place in heaven and came to earth with the purpose of becoming our Redeemer. His mission was not to condemn the world, but to redeem mankind and break the bondages of sin. By His death on the cross, Jesus paid the price for our release from sin and its consequences. That whoever believes in Him would never perish (John 3:16). The benefits of redemption include eternal life (Revelation 5:9-10), forgiveness of sins (Ephesians 1:7), adoption into God's family (Galatians 4:5-7), and freedom from the law's curse (Galatians 3:13).

When Joseph's brothers threw him into the cistern, they set in motion a series of actions that would lead Joseph to redeem Israel from possible death by starvation. Joseph suffered in bondage for thirteen years until he was able to redeem his family from the devastating effects of a famine. His sacrifices allowed God to position him and elevate him into a position of power and influence. In turn, he was able to bless his family with grain and eventually relocate them to the fertile land of Goshen. There, the family of seventy people prospered and eventually grew into a nation of over 1.5 million people in less than 400 years. This fulfilled the promise God gave Abram that his descendants would be more numerous than the stars (Genesis 17).

Previously, we learned that between the receipt of the dream or vision and the actual manifestation, there is a season of preparation. At the appropriate time, God will redeem the dream or vision. Don't worry or fret. The dream or vision you had to surrender in order to line up with the will of God will be redeemed, and all that you sacrificed will be restored.

Take for instance Abraham, Moses, Hannah, and Zechariah. In time, God redeemed their desires and prayers. Abraham waited twenty-five years for a son and Moses waited forty years to lead his people out of slavery. Hannah and Zechariah waited many years before God gave them children. God knows the desires of your heart as He did theirs. He blessed them in the end, and He will do the same for you.

Why Did It Take So Long?

Okay, this is the tough question. There have been many days when I found myself asking this exact question, *why did it take so long?* The answer came one day as I sat at my table working on this chapter. Some of the time was needed, because God was orchestrating things in the lives of other people for my benefit. The remainder of the time was required to prepare me. You see, when God opens a door through another person, I need to quickly walk through it. Reflecting back on my time in the wilderness, I see how my actions actually delayed my blessing. A missed conversation, taking the wrong opportunity, not moving when I was nudged to move all cost me delays in moving forward. Every error taught me important lessons about obedience and faith. Each setback taught me the importance of moving whenever I felt that nudge in my spirit. Over time, I learned to be still when my mind and my friends were screaming "Do something!" I learned to have discernment concerning who I allowed to speak into my life.

Unfortunately, not everyone who speaks into your life brings a word from God. The Enemy also sends messages to distract you from the true plan of God.

Why did it take so long? Partly because there were so many things I needed to learn. At the top of the list was speaking life over every situation, and moving toward my future by faith. I had to stop speaking doubt and curses over my life (emanating from my frustration level). The process taught me to trust God more than I trusted my natural abilities. It reminded me that His thoughts are not our thoughts and His ways are not our ways (Isaiah 55:8). Finally, I learned the futility of worrying about when things were going to happen. This chapter proved to be the most challenging to write, because it took some time for me to get the necessary revelation. But at the right time, revelation was released that allowed me to continue pressing forward.

Beyond what we can see, God is orchestrating events in the lives of other people so that at the right time, our interactions will achieve His desired purpose. It is not as simple as a genie blinking her eyes or snapping her fingers and granting our wish. Just to put this in perspective, if Isaac had been born ten years earlier, would he have married Rebecca? Or would he have settled for a Canaanite woman? If Joseph had been released from prison earlier, would he have had the opportunity to interpret Pharaoh's dream? If Ruth had abandoned Naomi when Orpah left, would she have married Boaz? In each of these stories, the individual persisted until God's promise came to pass.

The answer to the question of why so long is because we have to be available and in position when God moves in Kairos time. If you are struggling in this area, this may be a good time to tell your flesh to stop complaining about *when*. God's timing is not our timing. But know this, God's timing is perfect. Sounds like a good time to focus living in the now.

Will You Wait for God?

If you trust the Lord in all things, it should be easy waiting on His timing for redemption and restoration. If this is the case, why are you anxious about when God will restore you? Maybe this is what James was thinking about when he wrote that a double-minded man is unstable in all his ways (James 1:8).

Waiting on God has challenged many believers. Successfully overcoming this challenge requires surrendering your life to God's will and His perfect timing. Contrary to what your flesh may say, there are things for you to do while you wait. This is the time to work on transforming your mind by feeding on the Bread of Life. Our goal should be to exhibit the fruit of the Spirit in our daily actions. This will require submitting to the leading of the Holy Spirit.

Galatians 5:22-23 provides us with characteristics that Spirit-led believers will demonstrate. *But the fruit of the Spirit is love, joy, peace, longsuffering, gentleness, goodness, faith, meekness and temperance; against such there is no law* (KJV).

When believers follow the leading of the Holy Spirit, their actions and behaviors will reflect the virtues stated in this Scripture. I like the King James version because it uses the word longsuffering instead of patience. Longsuffering is a virtue that mature believers develop from enduring long seasons of trials and testing. Since God operates in Kairos time, recipients of the overflow blessing will have to endure for a season.

Moses spent forty years in the desert learning how to navigate and survive before God called him to lead the Hebrews out of Egypt. Hannah cried for years before she became pregnant with Samuel. Joseph waited over twenty-two years before he witnessed the manifestation of the two dreams. Despite how they felt about their circumstances, they all trusted God to come through for them.

Mature believers have learned that God is faithful, and His Word will not come back void. They have learned to wait on God's timing.

You have come too far to quit and return to that former life. You are going to make it. Continue doing all He has instructed you to do, because God's promises are yes and amen.

Restoration

What does it mean when God promises to restore something? Let's start by looking at the definition of the word. *Restore* means to bring back to a previous state, to return to a former condition, place, or position. Restoration is the process of bringing something back to its former state.

One day, a reality TV show caught my eye. Two restoration guys were searching through a collector's inventory of junk vehicles for rare gems. They spotted the grill of a vintage Ford truck covered with a dust-filled tarp. When they pulled the tarp back, they found the body and frame in good condition, with the original motor as well. They were excited by their find. They purchased the truck for $5,000 and transported it back to their shop. They spent the next several weeks restoring the vehicle and finally sold it at auction for $50,000 dollars.

It is fascinating that people will spend money to repair and refurbish old cars to their original splendor. Obviously, these two guys could see past the dirt, dents, and missing parts to see the real value of the car. They purchased one man's junk and meticulously restored it to become another man's treasure.

This is how God feels about His children. Your shortcomings and failures do not intimidate Him. He wants to restore you so you can be a living testimony of His divine grace and mercy. The sacrifices you made during the transformation process were not in vain. Once you have successfully completed the transformation process, God will release an overflow blessing that will make you forget about your past. He will prepare a table for you before your enemies, and your life will be restored before their eyes. Just like Joseph, you will experience prosperity in the land of your suffering.

And the God of all grace, who called you to his eternal glory in Christ, after you have suffered a little while, will himself restore you and make you strong, firm, and steadfast.
—1 Peter 5:10 NIV

Suddenly

One day while I was sitting at my kitchen table working on this chapter, the word *suddenly* dropped into my spirit. During the day, I continued to see the word in various places, and I could hear the word in my spirit. I recalled places in the Bible where I'd seen it.

- Suddenly, the walls of Jericho collapsed, and the Israelites rushed into the city.
- Suddenly, the sea parted before Moses, allowing the Israelites to escape the Egyptians.
- Suddenly, fire and brimstone rained down on Sodom and Gomorrah.
- Suddenly, Joseph was elevated into running the nation of Egypt.
- Suddenly, the Holy Spirit descended on the 120 waiting in the upper room.

The point is when God moves, everyone will know it was God,

because the movement is sudden. What would take man years to achieve, God can do in the blink of an eye. Don't allow the Enemy to discourage you with statements about how long it will take. You serve the God of the *now*. God moves in the right time, the perfect time. Be encouraged, it's not too late for you to receive the overflow blessing. You haven't missed it, nor have you disqualified yourself. When you have done all you can do, the only thing you can do is stand. Stand firm in your faith and watch the God of our salvation move in your life.

One of my favorite examples of suddenly is found in Exodus, Chapter 12. Before the last plague hit Egypt, Moses instructed the Hebrews to make preparations to leave, to mark their houses with blood, and to ask the Egyptians for articles of gold and silver upon their release. That night, the plague of the firstborn struck, and every house in Egypt was impacted except those with special blood markings on the door post. The grieving nation urged the Israelites to leave immediately and even offered them articles of clothing, gold, and silver for the exodus. The Israelites left with their livestock and the wealth of a powerful nation.

Once again, God moved mightily to bless a nation of over one million people with freedom and prosperity. In the span of twenty-four hours, they went from slavery to freedom, carrying the wealth of the most powerful nation of that time. In the blink of an eye, they catapulted from a season of just enough to a season of excess. There is a suddenness when God moves. Are you ready?

Matthew 25:1-13 sheds some critical insight on sudden manifestations of the overflow blessing. This is the parable of the ten virgins who were going out to meet the bridegroom. The five foolish ones took their lamps but no additional oil. The wise virgins took extra oil with their lamps, and they all waited for the bridegroom. After many hours, darkness fell. The virgins fell asleep. Around midnight, the bridegroom arrived, and they all rushed out to meet him.

The lamps of the five foolish virgins flickered as the oil ran out.

The foolish virgins had to go back for more oil. But the wise ones refilled their lamps from the oil they brought with them and went with the bridegroom to the wedding banquet. When the foolish ones returned a short time later, they were not allowed to enter the banquet. This parable illustrates one aspect of the overflow blessing. The door will open without warning, and only those who are prepared will be able to walk through it.

For Joseph, the door to the overflow blessing opened suddenly. With faith strengthened by a season of trials and testing, Joseph humbly stepped into the role of running a nation. He did not hesitate, nor did he request additional time to pray for direction. For him, the answer was easy. The source of his confidence was not in his natural abilities, but in God, who provided both direction and favor. He knew that the God who enabled him to endure slavery, to prosper in Potiphar's house and the prison, and to interpret dreams, would surely empower his success in Egypt.

What does this mean for the modern-day believer? The first sign of the overflow blessing will be everything happening all at once. There will not be any time for pondering your decision to move forward. You will have to step out on faith—the same faith that enabled you to endure the transformation process. From the outside, people will wonder how this blessing happened to you. But this is the nature of the blessing. From obscurity to visibility and prosperity. The Bible says, *those who exalt themselves will be humbled, and those who humble themselves will be exalted* (Matthew 23:12 NIV).

Continue walking by faith in the season you are in. Be receptive to changing under the guidance of the Holy Spirit. Make sure to embrace every learning opportunity so you will be fully prepared to walk into your open door.

No Looking Back

When the door of opportunity opens, you will face a momentous decision. There will be no instruction on how to navigate the new opportunity, nor will there be anyone to explain things in advance. Will you step out in faith and trust God to take care of the details? This is not the time to long for the comfort and security of your past life. Don't be like Lot's wife and lose out on your future. I wonder if she, like the Hebrew slaves, was more afraid of the unknown than the terrible conditions they had grown accustomed to.

Remember, the wilderness is not meant to be our final home. It is meant to prepare us to receive the blessing from God. As you prepare to step into your opportunity, here are five pitfalls you need to avoid.

1. Longing for the past.

2. Worrying about the how things will happen.

3. Comparing your situation to others.

4. Becoming intimidated by the sudden elevation.

5. Forgetting about the Holy Spirit.

In the book of Exodus, God moved mightily to demonstrate His power and supreme nature to the former Hebrew slaves. When facing new challenges, the people chose to murmur and complain instead of trusting their God. They had the audacity to long for the food and security of slavery instead of following God into the land filled with opportunities and hope. Longing for the past and worrying about the future opened the door which led to their disobedience, which ultimately doomed that generation to wander and die in the desert.

The lesson for modern believers is that it is impossible to move forward when you are always looking back at your past. Imagine how much progress you will make driving forward while constantly staring in the rearview mirror. That sounds like an accident waiting to happen.

When Pharaoh presented the opportunity to Joseph to run the

country, it was Joseph's only option for escaping the past. The isolation he experienced in the prison resulted in the elimination of all potential distractions. For Joseph, there was no plan B or C; he only had one choice. But his confidence in God suppressed any concern he had with talking to Pharaoh. He had been prepared his entire life for a time such as this.

Imagine going from slave labor to meeting the president of the United States to solve a problem that threatened the nation. There is no time to worry and panic. You have to step boldly into the new opportunity God has provided for you and trust Him to carry you through. This section only applies to those who trust the Lord. My editor says I should ask if you really trust God. Do you?

Because of our time in the wilderness, we know God is the source of our strength. He promises to guide our footsteps (via the Holy Spirit) as we walk in His will. Therefore, we will not be intimidated by the overflow blessing. Joseph did not hesitate when Pharaoh made him second in command, and neither will you. When you discern God opening the next door, throw caution to the wind and *jump* right in with both feet.

Summary

Hebrews 12:2 reminds us that God is the author and finisher of our faith. He has written the plan for our lives, and He will move on our behalf to bring it to fruition. The only thing we have to do is be obedient and walk in faith. Once He shares the vision with us, He will guide us to the manifestation if we faint not. At the right time, He will redeem the vision and restore all that was lost.

The story of Joseph illustrates the fundamental aspects of our Father. Joseph placed his trust solely in the Lord despite his circumstances. Unlike many of us, Joseph never allowed his problems to block his line of sight to God. By consistently seeking God's face, he was able to discern and stay in His will. The favor of God enabled him to experience success.

God was faithful to redeem Joseph's dreams and restore his life. He will do the same for those who have left the comfortable place, who have endured the preparation process, and experienced transformation in their lives. They will receive the blessing. Aligning our lives to His will opens the windows of heaven. Surrendering and walking in obedience avails believers to many heavenly riches. For those who will allow their lives to be transformed by God, they will walk in seasons of abundance and prosperity.

Just know that at the right time, God will redeem your vision or dream. He will accelerate you quickly into a new realm of existence filled with favor and opportunities. When the door opens, everything will happen suddenly.

Thankfully, the wilderness taught you how to overcome fear and doubt. It taught you not to long for what you had. When those anxious thoughts swirl in your mind, you have learned to focus on the author and finisher of your faith, Christ Jesus. You can achieve all things through Christ who strengthens you. You can boldly walk into the new opportunity and receive your overflow blessing.

Our God is faithful to finish the good work He has started in us. Losing is not an option for those who walk with God. If you identify your current situation as being in the transformation process, be confident in knowing that God will restore and redeem you at the right time.

Refection Questions

1. List two reasons that indicate you are ready for your dream opportunity.

2. Who do you need to forgive before you can fully walk into your overflow blessing?

3. List three things you learned about yourself during the transformation process?

4. What would you say to others while they are in the transformation process?

5. List any distractions that are causing you to take your focus off God's promise. What steps are you taking to eliminate them?

Meditation Scriptures

Jeremiah 29:11
Romans 15:13
Hebrews 12:2
Matthew 26:42

CHAPTER TEN

Surviving the Darkness

Many are the afflictions of the righteous: but the Lord delivereth him out of them all.

—Psalm 34:19 KJV

I LOVE TO go fishing early in the morning before sunrise. There is a wonderful peace that occurs in the last hour of the night. It is also the darkest time of the night.

One morning I literally could not see to tie a lure on my line. This reminds me of an old proverb that says "it is always darkest before the dawn." This natural phenomenon is also true for anyone pursuing an overflow blessing. The period immediately before the breakthrough will be the darkest period in your life.

This is the time when, despite your obedience and faithfulness, nothing is happening. The attacks of the Enemy are more vicious, and people all around you question your mental state just like Job's friends. Family members question if you are really hearing from God. *Surely God would not allow His chosen to suffer like you have.* Church members question your commitment to God. *It must be something you are doing wrong.* Those who are self-righteous will press you to confess your sins and repent. Some may go as far as Job's wife by telling you to curse God and die (Job 2:9). Meanwhile, the path forward is obscured by darkness.

During this time, you cling to the promise of God with all your strength. Surrounded by waning support, your focus shifts to your Creator. *Lord, if you don't make something happen, I am going to perish.* Your spirit shouts *hold on, don't quit now.* It senses the movement that has already happened in the heavens. It knows the right time of God is about to occur. But your flesh is weary because of the years of service and sacrifice. Those all around you are flourishing, but you continue to languish in the dry place. Your mind screams *have you forgotten about me Lord?* For the thousandth time, your mind reviews all God has instructed you to do to see if you missed something. The answer always comes back the same: *no, you haven't.*

I suspect Joseph experienced these same thoughts while in prison. *Lord, did you forget about me?* What kept him from giving up? What prevented him from losing his sanity? What stopped him from wanting to end his life? If this resonates with you, know you are closer than ever to your breakthrough.

When the Egyptian officials failed to remember Joseph after their release, he entered the darkest segment of his preparation season. Despite their promise to remember him, his hope faded with each passing week. Yet Joseph continued to exercise his prison responsibilities faithfully and cheerfully. Somehow, he managed to stay focused on God instead of his imprisonment. So can you. You have survived this long by standing on the Word of God. Your faith has enabled you to endure numerous trials and challenges. Let's look at harnessing the power of gratitude to thrive in this temporary season.

Gratitude Maintains Focus

Cultivating a spirit of gratitude is crucial for enduring the challenges of the preparation process. Teaching ourselves to be thankful for what we have shifts the focus away from what we don't have. Gratitude keeps our eyes on God, our provider, our protector, our comforter. Gratitude turns what we have into more than enough. When we operate in a spirit of gratitude, we are appreciative of random calls from friends, a stranger saying hello, reaching our destinations safely, having money in our pockets, and food in our cupboards. Gratitude allows us to sense the hand of God moving every day. It reminds us we are His valuable and precious children. When we operate in a spirit of gratitude, we find peace in any circumstance. The apostle Paul shared this principle in his letter to the church at Philippi.

I know what it is to be in need, and I know what it is to have plenty. I have learned the secret of being content in any and every situation whether well fed or hungry, whether living in plenty or in want. I can do all this through Him who gives me strength.
—Philippians 4:12-13 NIV

Paul wrote this because he understood that God alone was his source. His contentment emanated from what he fundamentally believed, that fellowshipping with God was greater than any temporal circumstances.

We must refrain from allowing temporary problems to obscure the Lord God Almighty and make every effort to cultivate a spirit of gratitude so we can maintain our focus on God. Operating with a spirit of gratitude will dampen our emotional swings and prevent delays caused by the words we speak. Most importantly, there is a wonderful blessing for those who sacrifice to see God's face. *You will keep in perfect peace those whose minds are steadfast, because they trust in you* (Isaiah 26:3 NIV).

It is easy to lose sight of these truths when the season of preparation stretches out over several years. The rising level of our frustration can block our view of God. We might still be serving Him at church, but we struggle to hear Him. If we are not cognizant to renew our minds daily, our hope can fade. Lacking His guidance, we soon depart from the good path He has for our lives. That is why the Enemy bombards us with negative thoughts concerning what we don't have. He knows that ungratefulness makes us vulnerable to taking our eyes off of God.

Don't let this happen to you. If you have drifted away, run back to your first love. He is there waiting for you.

Show me the right path, O Lord; point out the road for me to follow. Lead me by your truth and teach me, for you are the God who saves me. All day long I put my hope in you.
—Psalm 25:4-5 NLT

Blinded by Discontentment

The Enemy has one diabolical trap waiting for believers who are on the verge of a breakthrough. He loves to unleash the spirit of discontentment to agitate our emotions and inflame our pride. The dictionary defines *discontentment* to mean a lack of satisfaction with one's possessions, status, or situation. This spirit causes people to become disgruntled or displeased with where they are in life. Like many of the Enemy's weapons, its purpose is to distract us and get us to take our eyes off of God. The Enemy knows if he can get us off of God's path for our life, he can delay God's blessing.

When people are snared by the spirit of discontentment, they constantly complain about their circumstances. They are never satisfied with what they have. They are always looking for something else. You know the type. The husband with a loving, nurturing wife who longs for a size six model. The wife with a faithful, hardworking, husband who longs for a lean, muscular biker dude struggling to make child-support payments. An employee wants to be the boss, because it pays more. The boss wants to be the employee, because of less headaches and responsibilities. It's funny how one person will complain about their half-full glass, whereas the thirsty man rejoices at the mere sight of water.

When this spirit of discontentment strikes, people stop praising God for what they have. They question why they don't have this and that. Complaining shifts to blaming God, which results in communicating less with God. When this happens, we veer off the path God had for us and ultimately wander aimlessly in the wilderness.

Don't be deceived and fall into this subtle trap. This spirit will not attack your relationship with God. It will focus on the delayed manifestation of the promise. Its goal is to erode your hope in the promise. Left by itself, this spirit is simply a minor irritant. But this sinister spirit loves to lull believers into lowering their guard (by complaining), which opens the door for other spirits to attach themselves—spirits such as anger, depression, envy, jealousy, bitterness, and anxiety.

Thankfully, this can all be averted by renewing our minds daily with the Word of God. This enables us to cast down every thought and imagination that is contrary to the Word. If you find yourself feeling hopeless because the promise has not happened, then you are putting your hope in the wrong place. As mature believers, we should always place our hope in the Lord God Almighty, the Creator of all there is.

Luke 1:37 reminds us that nothing is impossible for God. He alone is faithful to complete what He has started in us. And His promise will come to fruition for those who complete the entire process. Joseph completed the process and received an incredible overflow blessing. Know that God wants to do the same for you.

Living in the Now

One of the keys to maintaining a balanced perspective during the preparation season is learning to live in the now. Life is more enjoyable when you maximize this concept. Living in the now means not dwelling on the past and not worrying about the future. Stop regurgitating past failures every week. Stop pulling the scab off old emotional wounds and wondering why certain people treated you the way they did. Stop replaying old discussions and wondering what could have happened. Whenever you think about the past, stop and reflect on how God has allowed you to see this day. Releasing the past and learning to be grateful for each day helps you live in the now. "Let today be the day you gave up who you've been for who you can become" (Hal Elrod).

What is the purpose of worrying about next year, next month, or next week? Why model various scenarios in our mind of things that have yet to happen? If God can deliver us from our past, He can certainly take care of our future.

How many of you realize that we can make things out to be worse in our minds than they really are? Those things will take care of themselves at the appropriate time. Worrying about tomorrow will cause us to lose precious time living today. "The bridges you cross before you come to them are over rivers that aren't there" (Gene Brown). Does this quote apply to you?

The Enemy loves to distract believers by reminding us of our past. His objective is to take our focus off of God and put it on our circumstances. At the right time, he will send suggestions and thoughts that will cause us to pause and reflect. When we contemplate our past, he bombards us with negative thoughts that make us question our self-worth or, worse, bring condemnation.

What happens next is inevitable. Our flesh kicks in and rationalizes why we are not worthy to receive anything from God. If this attack goes on too long, it will sap our resolve and the energy required to persevere. It will drain our excitement for the journey and cause us to long for the familiar place. When our spirit finally breaks, we abort the journey and forfeit our blessing.

The Enemy's attacks can be thwarted with the right rebuke. Though it is simple and will cost you nothing, it is something that must be done often. Pure and simple, you must learn to rebuke the Enemy by saying *my past does not dictate my future.* And another thing. Refrain from idolizing the past and rehearsing painful memories. The Lord wants to do a new thing in your life. Will you receive it? In his book *Now What,* Dr. Francis Myles shares some great advice for living in the now. "Don't let your conscious park in the past," he says. "Instead, drive it into the present, and pull up the parking break."

Joseph gives us a wonderful example of how to live in the now. He excelled in every situation he faced. The first thing we notice is that he did not long for the past. He did not murmur or complain about missing his family. He did not complain to other slaves about losing his freedom unfairly. Nor did he fret about his future. He did not tell everyone his dreams. He focused on living in the now where he turned people's problems into successes that glorified God.

When I was going through a wilderness period, I struggled with living in the now. I alternated between complaining about doors that God closed and doors He had yet to open. I constantly worried about how I was going to survive. Fortunately, I had a few friends who constantly reminded me to enjoy each day. They would listen to me complain and worry about not having a job. They were so patient with me. In retrospect, they could see the hand of God molding my life. He had separated me from the comfortable place and was preparing me for my overflow blessing. They continued to speak affirming words over me. I am grateful God placed those encouragers in my life. Without a doubt, those words provided precious drops of water when I was in the middle of the preparation, which seemed more like a desert than an oasis of comfort.

Eventually, I grasped this concept of living in the present and implemented it into my daily habits. This simple principle significantly improved my attitude and my perspective. Learning to live in the now allowed me to be more productive as well as more supportive of others in their journey to their own blessing.

In order to enjoy living in the now, you must trust God's plan for your day. This will require listening for His instructions and guidance during your daily prayer time. Unfortunately, many of us neglect our daily instructions, because we are too focused on achieving the vision. When we spend time listening for His voice rather than telling Him what we want, our interaction shifts from a monologue to a conversation. We wake up with anticipation for knowing what God's plan is for that day. With Jesus as both Lord and Savior, we have confidence knowing He will provide our daily bread. *Do not be anxious about anything, but in every situation, by prayer and petition, with thanksgiving, present your requests to God* (Philippians 4:6 NIV).

Let me share ten tips for living in the now.

1. *Pray for your daily assignment.*

2. *Find something to be grateful for each day.*

3. *Celebrate daily victories.*

4. *Learn from your past, but do not live in it.*

5. *Embrace the hope of your vision, and do not worry about the how.*

6. *View every situation as a learning opportunity.*

7. *Stop glorifying the Enemy with your words.*

8. *Remember that God is bigger than your challenges.*

9. *Speak life into people, independent of the situation.*

10. *Commit to memorizing a Scripture every week.*

Finally, staying grateful will make it easier to live in the now. Imagine how you would behave if tomorrow's blessing was dependent on what you were grateful for today. Would you spend as much time complaining about what you don't have? The Bible says both life and death are in the power of the tongue (Proverbs 18:21). I guess that is why my grandmother used to say "if you can't say anything nice, don't say anything at all." The following quote summarizes the importance of having a spirit of gratitude. "Gratitude makes sense of the past, brings peace for today, and creates vision for tomorrow" (Melody Beattle).

Honoring God in Our Wait

Waiting on God's timing can be extremely challenging. because it seems like nothing is going on. Yet even in our wait, we play a crucial role in advancing God's kingdom on earth.

The wilderness season has taught us how to operate in the will of God. How we behave while we wait is very important. When we look at Joseph, he continued trusting the God of his dream despite being forgotten. He continued to manage the prison with excellence, and the favor of the Lord rested upon him. How many people can make a similar claim? Filled with the glory of God, Joseph served as a living witness to everyone in the prison. In his daily tasks, people saw a glimpse of the living God. The same holds true for us today.

Nowadays, people scrutinize Christians to see if we are living what we profess to believe. They watch our response to challenges and difficulties. They expect us to respond with emotional outbursts, incessant complaining, and blame-shifting. But when our behaviors reflect the Word that resides inside of us, the outside world sees something different. Instead of viewing our sinful flesh, they see us calm and making positive affirmations about our situation. They see Christ operating in us. When we are obedient to God's Word, it transforms us into His image.

Don't allow the lies of the Enemy to deceive you. You are fulfilling a kingdom purpose even while you wait on the manifestation of the blessing. You can be an effective witness to people who are going through similar situations. By sharing your story, you can sow seeds of encouragement that enable others to continue running their race. They can draw strength from watching how you endured similar challenges.

How do people see you in this time of your life? Do they see a steadfast person of faith living in the now of each day? Or do they see a discontent person struggling with doubt and unbelief? Will they see an obedient servant of God or someone struggling with fleshly desires? When bad things happen, will they see the love of Christ, or will they experience the wrath of your flesh? Everything you do and say communicates which kingdom you serve. Can people tell that you serve the risen Lord? The apostle Paul summarized this best in the following Scripture: *So whether you eat or drink, or whatever you do, do it all for the glory of God* (1Corinthians 10:31 NIV).

The key to maintaining strength while you wait is to continually be in communion with God. According to Paul, when we are weak, He is strong. In 2 Corinthians 12:9, Jesus said, *my grace is sufficient for you, for my power is made perfect in weakness* (NIV). He will undergird our faith while we wait. He will keep in perfect peace all who are focused on him. According to Isaiah 40, the Lord *gives strength to the weary and increases the power of the weak* (vs. 29).

Don't despair about your situation. The Lord is working on your behalf to bring about a blessed outcome.

Don't Lose Hope

In the fall of 2018, I lost a friend due to suicide. At the funeral, everyone was shocked by the untimely death. Later, I found out my friend had suffered some recent setbacks and had simply lost hope. This hit me hard, because I was in a dark period in my life, and my own hope was fading. But something prevented me from entertaining thoughts about quitting. God had brought me too far to leave me. That experience motivated me to write this chapter. Maintaining our hope is critical for surviving in this period. How do we maintain hope during challenging times? Let's look at the story of King David for insight.

The book of Psalms reveals the intimate relationship David had with the Lord. Although David was a mighty man of valor, he was totally dependent on God for his strength. Whenever David faced trouble, he sought out God's face. His hope rested in God. In Psalm 25:5 David wrote, *Guide me in your truth and teach me, for you are God my Savior, and my hope is in you all day long* (NIV).

In order for God to guide and teach him, David had to make Him a priority in his life. David was able to renew his hope and faith by spending time with God. The same holds true for believers today. If the charge on your faith battery is getting low, it's time to plug in to the source of your hope. Did you seek God's face before you started your day today?

Let me address those who are struggling to have hope. I found myself in this place when I was writing this chapter. While quitting was not an option, my hope was wavering, and it seemed like I was slipping back into my old ways. The Holy Spirit revealed the key to maintaining hope one day while I was playing for a soaking worship session. Fading hope is an indication of not spending enough time in God's presence. It results from looking at our circumstances more than our deliverer. Spending time daily with my heavenly Father recharged my batteries and renewed my hope.

In order to maintain our hope, we must press deeper into our worship and prayer time. Like David, we have to fervently seek God until we find Him. Psalm 62:5 says, *Yes, my soul, find rest in God; my hope comes from Him* (NIV).

Now that we understand how to renew our hope, what about our joy? Again, the answer can be found spending time in God's presence. The Bible says in Acts 2:28, *You have made known to me the paths of life; you will fill me with joy in your presence* (NIV). For me, spending quality time with God refreshed my hope and filled me with His unfailing love. This allowed me to conduct kingdom business by ministering to the people He showed me. God wants to use you even in this season to be a blessing to others. You have been bought with a price (1 Corinthians 6:20). Will you choose His will over your flesh?

Who Do You Trust?

The life of King David illustrates the ongoing struggle between the spirit man and the carnal man. Time and again, we see David high in the Lord one minute and then battling his flesh the next. Fortunately for us, the book of Psalms captures the discussions David had with the Lord during his challenging seasons. When faced with doubts and uncertainty, David consistently ran back to the Lord for assurance and guidance. In Psalm 28:7, David wrote, *The Lord is my strength and my shield; my heart trusted in him, and I am helped* (NKJV). David trusted God more than he trusted mortal man.

The question for the day is who do you trust?

In this season of waiting, how many of us can align with David on this matter? I fear that some saved and sanctified people are desperately looking for a word from man instead of trusting in God. Some are praying for a prophetic word to satisfy their carnal minds. Some are running to their saved friends for a word. Others have sought out false gods such as alcoholism and drugs to dull their senses and provide a brief respite from their ongoing frustration.

If you are struggling in this season, maybe it's time to make a decision. Either you will trust the Lord or you will trust your flesh. There will be no peace until that decision is made. *Blessed is the one who trusts in the Lord, who does not look to the proud, to those who turn aside to false gods* (Psalm 40:4 NIV).

Who do you really trust? Have you placed all your trust in yourself or God? Does your pride govern who you trust? Does it prevent you from trusting the God you cannot see? The funny thing is God is looking at you to determine if He can trust you. Humility is all about trusting God more than you trust yourself. When we operate in humility, obedience becomes an afterthought. What was once a difficult struggle becomes simple, because we have placed our trust in God to guide our footsteps.

Let me share a simple truth. There is freedom in trusting the sovereign Lord. You don't have to worry about what is going to happen. All you have to do is what He tells you, and that takes off all the pressure. You don't have to worry or fret. Just be obedient, knowing He has each day planned out for you. Simply seek His face each day, receive your instructions, and then operate in them. He will give you everything you need to be successful for that day. No need to stress yourself out worrying about possibilities, just focus on enjoying every day of life.

If you are struggling to have peace living in the now, ask God to search your heart and highlight areas where you may not be fully trusting Him. Once they have been identified, release them to God through prayer, and allow Him to deliver you.

Hidden for a Season

There will come a time in your journey when God will hide you for a season. He takes this action not to punish you, but to protect you. If you are experiencing a period of closed doors and failing relationships, you are being isolated on purpose. God has hidden you from the Enemy and any distractions that would lead you away from the path of your destiny. You have grown significantly during the preparation process, and now you are waiting on God to open the next door.

For me, this was a very challenging time, because my flesh was screaming to do something. Some days I found myself looking at engineering jobs on the Internet, even though I knew that door had been closed. My impatience made me susceptible to settling for the *good* thing when God wanted to give me the *great* thing. Our frustration signals to the Enemy that we are vulnerable to distractions and counterfeits. God anticipates this and hides us outside the reach of our enemies. *For in the day of trouble He will keep me safe in His dwelling, He will hide me in the shelter of His sacred tent and set me high upon a rock* (Psalm 27:5).

When God hides you, things will be happening all around you, but you will not be able to participate. It may feel like some invisible force is stopping you from making things happen. For example, you will find plenty of jobs that need your skillset, but no one will interview you. There will be church activities that would benefit from your knowledge, but you are never invited to participate. The people you helped over the years are not assisting you now.

Don't worry, God has not forgotten about you. God hid David for years when Saul wanted to kill him. God hid Moses in the desert for nearly forty years before calling him to deliver the Hebrews out of slavery in Egypt. He hid newly converted Paul for three years before releasing him into his ministry. He hid me on and off for six years in order for me to complete this book. But rest assured, at the right moment He will lead you out of obscurity. Continue striving daily to be the best disciple of Christ you can be.

The Badge of Humility

For those who have submitted to the Lord Jesus Christ, humility is the evidence of spiritual maturity. Christians who have endured the wilderness season seek to serve others rather than being served. They follow the pattern established by their Lord and Savior. Jesus humbled himself by taking the form of man and suffering physical death in obedience to His father's will. His life provides us with a perfect picture of humility.

Like Christ, the humble believer values the importance of others more than self. A humble believer does not boast or promote self. They are always working behind the scenes to make things happen. They have a quiet confidence, because they understand they can do all things in Christ Jesus. Choosing God's will for their lives has set them free from worry, doubt, and anxiety. Instead of trying to figure out things on their own, they allow God to guide them explicitly. Instead of saying "I will," they say "He will." They constantly acknowledge that God is sovereign in their lives. Are you one of those people?

There are tremendous benefits from operating in humility. Because of the law of sowing and reaping, humble people tend to attract blessings. The Bible says the Lord will sustain the humble (Psalm 147:6 NIV) and show them favor (James 4:6 NIV). He gives wisdom to those who accept God's guidance (Psalm 25:9 NIV) and mercy to those who deserve judgement (1 Kings 21:29 NIV). He promises to save the humble (2 Samuel 22:38 NIV) and elevate them in due season (Luke 14:41 NIV). Wisdom, grace, and peace rest upon them, and the joy of the Lord overflows in them. Although enemies plot to destroy them, God delivers them from all snares and pitfalls. Proverbs 22:4 says, *Humility is the fear of the Lord; its wages are riches and honor and life* (NIV).

Why do so many people struggle to achieve humility in their lives? Why is the spirit of pride running rampant in the body of believers? The answer is simple. Humility is the sign of someone who has completely surrendered their life to Christ. In order for this to happen, pride and love of self must die. Unfortunately, this will disqualify many believers.

There is power for those who operate in humility. There is freedom from pride and arrogance, because we recognize the inadequacies of the flesh. No matter the situation, we don't have to defend ourselves, because the Lord promises to fight our battles. Each day we put on the armor and stand confidently, because victory is assured. By operating in love, we bridge the gap that separates people and brings peace. We are comfortable in who we are and okay staying in our lane.

When we learn to serve, we tap into the power of humility. Matthew 5:5 says, *Blessed are the meek, for they shall inherent the earth* (NIV). The Greek word for meek is *praus,* which means gentle, humble, or mild. They used this word to describe a wild horse that had been brought under control.

The meek are people who have their strengths under control. Disciples of Christ have learned to sacrifice their flesh daily to do the will of the Father. They utilize their gifts and talents to conduct kingdom work on earth. They understand that God is fighting their battles. Even when it feels like they are surrounded by the Enemy, they know God is surrounding them. When God sees them serving others faithfully, He moves on their behalf to bless them. This is how the law of sowing and reaping is fulfilled. Romans 8:31 reminds us that *if God is for us, who can be against us* (NIV). For those whose pride will not allow God to direct their steps, I hope they enjoy wandering around in the wilderness.

Did you wear your humility badge today?

How Deep is Your Love?

The Christian journey involves many challenges designed to teach us about trusting God. But at some point, God will go quiet in order to determine if He can trust us. This is a time when there is no progress toward our destiny, and God is not communicating any new instructions. We have to obey the last set of instructions and stand firm by faith. This is not punishment. It is designed to determine the state of our heart. This is a time for God to see how deep our love is for him. He wants to see if we will stand faithfully or revert back to our self-centered ways?

When the manifestation of God's promise is not visible in our lives, will we continue to hope and walk in faith? Can we endure a season of no progress by our faith alone? Will we continue being faithful in our church, our families, and our communities despite going through a long dry season? While these are difficult questions, our answers will determine our maturity level as disciples of Christ. Will we love obeying God more than obeying our flesh?

Reflection Questions

1. What are you grateful for today? This week? This month?

2. What have you done to glorify God this week?

3. Do you know someone who you would call humble? List 2-3 characteristics they display in their everyday actions.

4. What actions are you taking to protect hope and strengthen your faith?

5. What steps have you taken to live in the now?

Meditation Scriptures

Psalm 34
Psalm 28:7
Psalm 40:1-2
James 4:6

CHAPTER ELEVEN

God is Faithful

For the Word of the Lord is right and true; He is faithful in all he does.

—Psalm 33:4 NIV

WEBSTER'S DICTIONARY DEFINES faithful as "steadfast in affection or allegiance, firm in adherence to promises, true to a standard or to an original copy." The word implies loyalty, consistency, and repeatability. When we say God is faithful, we are saying He is dependable and worthy of our trust. His Word will always come to fruition in His divine timing. The challenge for the believer is having patience and trusting the author of our faith.

In these latter days, the word faithful seems archaic in many ways. For instance, most large companies are no longer loyal to their workers. They are purging out older workers in order to bring in younger and cheaper labor. They cut benefits and freeze salaries while giving double-digit raises to top executives. Modern workers are seldom faithful to their employers. They hop from company to company in search of new opportunities that pay more money.

Employment is not the only arena where faithfulness is an archaic concept. The divorce rate is at an all-time high, because people are not faithful to their marriage covenant. The same holds true in government. Politicians and leaders promise one thing only to do another. In the age of instant gratification, the selfish desires or needs of the individual outweigh the promise of being faithful to his/her word to another. In short, people make promises with no intention of honoring them. Thankfully, the God of Abraham, Isaac, and Jacob is faithful to fulfill His promises, which are always yes and amen. *God is not human, that he should lie, not a human being, that he should change his mind. Does he speak and then not act? Does he promise and not fulfill?* (Numbers 23:19 NIV).

The annals of history are filled with people who have experienced God's faithfulness. Consider the examples of Abraham, Moses, Gideon, Ester, David, Samuel, Jeremiah, Peter, and Paul. Despite their shortcomings, they all stood on the promises of God and stepped out on faith to fulfill their respective destinies.

You are not alone in what you are going through. The founding fathers of America walked by faith to pen the Constitution and the Declaration of Independence. If you were to ask them about the key to their success, they would point back to their trust in God. In the face of uncertainty and doubt, they chose to operate by faith instead of surrendering to anxiety and despair. The question for you today is do you believe He is faithful?

If you are struggling to answer this question, you may be listening to the same source that told the ten Hebrew spies the promised land was bad. I saw the following quote on Facebook that speaks to where we all are at some point in our journey of faith. "Everything you are going through is preparing you for what you asked for" (Unknown).

From the story of Joseph, we know the path to the overflow blessing will require trusting God and obeying His will. It's funny how God will give you a snapshot of your future but will not reveal any of the obstacles and challenges you will face on the journey. I suspect if many of us knew what we had to endure in advance, we would walk away from the vision. But the vision speaks to the promises of God for those who will follow His guidance. Our faith becomes the conduit through which God's divine instructions flow. When we follow His guidance *in faith*, He is faithful to deliver His promise.

Anthony and Nicole were the proud parents of two healthy, vibrant boys. They were excited about raising their children in a loving Christian home. When friends brought up the topic of having more children, they quickly dismissed the subject. From their perspective, the family was complete. But God had other plans. Over time, He spoke to Nicole about having a daughter. She had dreams about a little girl at different ages. When she asked the Lord what that meant, He told her this was her daughter. During the same time, she received prophetic words from friends and strangers about having a daughter. After much prayer, Anthony and Nicole agreed to try again and were soon blessed with another son. Confused and discouraged, Nicole cried out. "Lord, didn't you say I was going to have a girl?"

The Enemy bombarded her with seeds of doubt. *Did God really say that? Did you really hear from God?* But Nicole continued seeking the Lord and serving Him. After receiving more confirming words, the couple struggled by faith through two heartbreaking miscarriages. When they finally stopped trying to conceive, God blessed them with a healthy baby girl. Now, they share their testimony with others about the faithfulness of God. He made a way when everything seemed impossible.

Don't despair, God's Word will not come back void. He will never leave or forsake you. Continue to walk by faith and rest in His promises.

He gives strength to the weary and increases the power of the weak. Even youths grow tired and weary, and young men stumble and fall; but those who hope in the Lord will renew their strength. They will soar on wings like eagles; they will run and not grow weary, they will walk and not be faint.

—Isaiah 40:28-31 NIV

Nothing Wasted

In the kingdom of God, everything has purpose, including trials and tests. They teach us to persevere by faith and place our trust solely in God. When you have walked with God long enough, you understand that nothing is wasted in His divine plan. The pain, suffering, and disappointment you experienced during the transformation process will be redeemed. One day you will find yourself ministering to people in situations similar to what you have gone through. That's when you receive the revelation of why God allowed you to go through the trials.

I once heard a sermon by a pastor who said your ministry can be found in your suffering. He reasoned that a person cannot speak on the healing powers of God if they have never been sick. People cannot tell others God is a provider if they have never had to depend on His provision. He ended his sermon with this deep, thought-provoking question. "How can you brag about His grace and mercy if you have never been forgiven for some horrible act?" Nothing is wasted. Everything happens for the good of His chosen people.

Looking back over my life, I can see how each challenge was designed to teach me about the magnificent nature of God. The times when God allowed things to happen to get me to move out of the comfortable place. The times when I walked in favor that I did not earn. The times when I endured setbacks so that one day I could be a blessing to others. The days when all I could do was stand in faith and place my trust in God. The days when not enough somehow provided all I needed. The days when the fiery attacks did not overwhelm and consume who I had become in Christ.

Those days and times were all part of God's plan. They played a critical role in building the foundation upon which my destiny would be erected. God is faithful, even when we don't reciprocate faithfulness. Let's examine the last part of Joseph's story to see how God used a bad thing to accomplish a great thing.

When Joseph returned from burying his father in the land of Canaan, his brothers worried that Joseph would take revenge against them (Genesis 50). Out of caution, they sent him a message containing Jacob's last wish. The message instructed Joseph to forgive his brothers for their sins. When Joseph read the message, he was moved to tears. Shortly afterward, the brothers came to him and, in obedience, fell at his feet shouting that they were his slaves. Joseph's response summarizes a key learning point for believers. *You intended to harm me, but God intended it for good to accomplish what is now being done, the saving of many lives* (Genesis 50:20 NIV).

Joseph understood that God had orchestrated everything in his life just for that moment. Each challenge served to position and prepare him for the day when he would lead a nation and simultaneously save his family from starvation. All of the negative experiences prepared him to operate in the overflow blessing. When he saw his brothers for the first time in years, the spirit of compassion overcame any desire to seek revenge. Everything worked according to the plan God had put in place, and nothing was wasted.

The same holds true for you. All the hardships, disappointments, and pain happened for a reason. The things you are going through *right now* are preparing you to move into your destiny. Your sacrifices are not in vain. You haven't wasted time and opportunities. When God moves in your life, every experience will be redeemed.

- The tears you shared gave you compassion for others.

- The times you spoke life over your enemies taught you how to dispense grace.

- The times you confessed your sins taught you to be merciful.

- The disappointments and setbacks taught you perseverance.

- The times you moved by faith taught you about God's faithfulness.

- The suffering taught you about the depth of the Father's love.

- The trials allowed you to purge impurities from your character.

- The battles taught you to stand and let God be God.

- Leaving the comfortable place taught you about faith.

- Crucifying your flesh allowed you to receive God's heart.

- Isolation made you sensitive to the voice of God.

- Losing everything taught you to be grateful for each day.

- Sowing into others taught you the power of the seed.

- Supporting another's vision prepared you to walk out your own.

- Controlling your emotions enabled you to walk in peace.

- Speaking life stopped you from cursing yourself.

Nothing is wasted in the kingdom of God. Everything that has happened in your life had a purpose. It has prepared you to walk in blessings that exceed anything you have imagined or dreamed about. Despite what your flesh thinks, you are exactly where you are supposed to be. I pray that the following Scripture resonates in your spirit.

Blessed is the one who perseveres under trial, because having stood the test, that person will receive the crown of life that the Lord has promised to those who love Him.

—James 1:12 NIV

Walking in God's Favor

When you are walking in the overflow blessing, God's favor abounds in your life. In this season, the difficult things become easy, and closed doors begin to open. You will experience an acceleration in your journey toward purpose and destiny. People will seek out your expertise to solve challenging problems. Resources in the form of money, time, and people will find and assist you. The season of *just enough* will morph into a season of *more than enough*. As a result, you will be able to bless others from your abundance. However, there is one small challenge with the timing of God's favor.

When God changes your season, there will be little advance notice. The transition from drought to prosperity will occur suddenly. Within a short period of time, the rain will start, and your land will blossom with new opportunities. There will be no time to prepare. You will have to move quickly through the open doors. Fortunately, the time in the wilderness taught you to overcome your fears by having faith in God. You will be able to confidently walk through the open door, because God is with you. But you must be prepared to receive the blessing so you are not consumed by it.

This next statement is not intended to dampen your spirit, but I feel I need to throw caution to wind: the overflow blessing will only magnify what is already in your heart. Any lingering character flaws will negatively impact your foundation. When you move to the next level, the settling foundation will cause cracks to appear in your house. Worse, whatever character issues you take into the next level will be magnified by an order of magnitude. With that disclaimer out of the way, let's get back on topic.

The favor upon Joseph's life extended to all who were associated with him. When Pharaoh heard that Joseph's brothers had come to Egypt, he blessed them with great favor. He told them to load up their animals and return to the land of Canaan to bring back the rest of their family members. He promised to give them the best land in Egypt and assured them they would enjoy the fat of the land (that's Bible speak for prosperity). He even gave them carts to bring back the people and told them to leave their possessions behind in Canaan *because the best of all Egypt will be yours* (Genesis 45:20). When the family left Canaan, they traveled to the fertile plains of Goshen where they settled. The seventy eventually became a nation of over one million people.

How many destiny chasers are ready to walk in God's favor? Are you truly ready to receive the overflow blessing God has for you?

Trust the Process

Eric's gift of organization enabled him to excel at managing complex problems. After graduating from college, he worked his way up from a mechanical draftsman to a project engineer position. Over the years, he developed an impressive track record implementing complex projects involving the design, construction, and installation of high-speed manufacturing equipment. When the country's economic bubble burst in 2001, contracts dried up for the automation company he worked for. Fortunately, Eric was able to switch into the medical device manufacturing market, which was experiencing double-digit growth.

Soon, he was successfully managing multi-million-dollar projects resulting in a high demand for his services. This was a benefit for his employer who reaped the financial windfall from Eric's work. Unfortunately, they were reluctant to share the profits with Eric.

In the midst of this successful time, God hatched a seed in Eric that would eventually manifest into him being a successful entrepreneur.

Despite his success, he struggled to find peace in a toxic workplace environment ruled by petty office politics. Despite his best efforts, Eric realized he did not belong in that culture. Little did he know God was training him for something bigger. One day he heard a message at his church that caused him to change his thinking.

For the next year, Eric engaged in discussions with mentors concerning stepping out and starting his own business. As the antics at work continued, God opened a door for Eric to step out on faith and start his business with a contract assignment in Cleveland, Ohio. That door closed after three months, and he found himself in a desperate place. Faced with the prospects of being broke, with a wife and a newborn child, Eric sowed an offering to the Lord out of desperation.

A few days later, he received a number of calls from prospective clients. He soon secured a large contract working for an international company. The company was in serious trouble with a regulatory body and in danger of being shut down. They were desperate for his expertise and willing to pay a premium price for his services. Eric was able to stabilize the client's business and get it back on track. Subsequently, the company gave him additional contracts to run other projects. In a few short years, Eric was able to add staffing, and his profitability quickly exceeded that of his former employers.

Eric had received the overflow blessing. Through his faithful obedience, God led Eric into a new promised land flowing with the proverbial milk and honey. In a short time, he went from being an undervalued employee to a thriving and prosperous business owner.

On a humorous note, his previous employer continues to actively recruit Eric with executive positions hoping he will return. It seems they finally realized the significant value he brought to the business. God used adversity to move Eric out of his familiar place in corporate America to position him to have a strategic conversation with a company that was desperate for his unique skills and abilities. Who knows, maybe God will direct Eric to purchase his previous employer's company.

God is still moving and doing wonderful things for those who trust Him and who obey his voice. What is He telling you to leave behind?

Surviving the Attack

The Enemy understands the importance of faith, and he makes it the primary target of his attacks. He knows God moves when faith is present, and he knows that without faith, it is impossible to please God (Hebrews 11:6). He will constantly assault your faith with negative thoughts and half-truths. If you have received a vision from God, just know that the Enemy has taken notice and will seek to discourage and frustrate you. He knows he cannot stop a move of God, but what he can do is influence you to abort God's plan yourself.

Here's something else the Enemy knows—our weaknesses and our tendencies. He has studied our reaction to different situations and knows our hot buttons. His arsenal of weapons can include anything from cantankerous co-workers, liars, and haters, to seductive distractions, comforting alcohol, numbing drugs, and so on. His goal is to distract us to either quit the process, settle for a distraction, or stop moving. All are designed to ensnare us with either the lust of the flesh, lust of the eye, or the pride of life (I John 2:16).

Many righteous believers have abandoned the race with the finish line in sight because of issues that have hurt their pride. Pride will cause us to stop moving, because we feel we deserve better. Pride will cause us to respond to our emotions, thus opening the door for a full assault by the Enemy. Pride will cause us to turn our back on the God who can save us. Pride is extremely dangerous, because it places self above God.

Let's shed some light on three common lies the Enemy loves to use to seduce the believer's faith. They are always sown in seed form as a thought or idea. Once we begin to constantly think about the lie, it opens the door for doubt and anxiety to come and rob the believer of peace. The good news is once the lie has been identified, it can be quickly defeated.

God is Blessing Everyone Else but Me

When you are deep in your wilderness, there will come a time when you will invariably notice people being blessed all around you. This observation should not surprise you, because the seasons for planting and harvesting are different for each person. While you can see the tangible fruit of that person's blessing, you cannot determine how long ago the seeds were sown.

Be careful. There is danger in trying to compare your journey with others. Watching people prosper and enjoy life while you are struggling will cause great stress and consternation if your heart is not right. By that, I mean when our heart is pure (free from jealousy, animosity, or lust), we can celebrate with others despite what we are experiencing. When the heart is tainted, jealousy and envy can emerge and rob our joy and peace. If you find yourself having negative thoughts about people being blessed, that is a sign of hidden iniquities in you. You will need to address this before it manifests into a bigger problem later. Remember, pride comes before a fall. *Humble yourselves before the Lord, and He will lift you up in honor* (James 4:10 NLT).

Someone Is Going to Steal My Destiny

The plan God has for you is just for you, no one else. Only you can walk the path to your destiny. The Enemy wants you to believe that people are out to steal your future. He wants you to believe you are not righteous enough for God to grant you full access to the destiny He planned for you.

Let me assure you that you *are* good enough. Stop believing the seeds of doubt the Enemy plants in your mind. And stop trying to walk in someone else's shoes. They will not fit, and you will hurt yourself trying to walk in them. Resist being anxious to experience your turn at success. In fact, replace any trace of anxiety with prayer and supplication by making your requests known to God (Philippians 4:6). Then wait patiently with an expectation for answers and direction. Besides, those who attempt to steal your destiny will be challenging the Almighty God. Guess who is going the win that fight?

God Has Forgotten About Me

Now we come to lie number three. This is one of the Enemy's favorite weapons to use against those who are struggling to be patient. He will wait for you to start verbalizing your frustration and disappointment before he whispers, *Are you sure you heard from the Lord? If so, why isn't anything happening. Looks like He has forgotten about you. You know you were not good enough anyhow. You should just quit and go back to what you used to do.*

If not careful, you will find yourself agreeing with his explanation of why you are *not* experiencing good times like everyone else. You may find yourself talking about all the reasons why God should not deliver on His promises. The Enemy slips away smiling, because he has shifted your focus away from God's faithfulness. This lie only works when we stop spending quality time with God.

Overcoming this lie may require using our special weapon. Worship energizes and strengthens our faith. Worship is not for Sunday service only. We can worship our God anytime we choose. When we worship, positive energy resonates through our body, impacting the condition of our heart. It moves the problem out of our view and replaces it with the God of the solution. Taking these actions will allow us to sense the presence of God again so we can say, *Okay, calm down, things are not that bad. He is here with me, and He hasn't forgotten about me. Let me continue running this race.*

Surviving the Enemy's attacks will require winning the battle for the mind. He is constantly attacking our thoughts and beliefs in order to persuade us to abort the process. Each day we must engage in active defense that casts down negative thoughts and replaces them with God's Word for our respective situations. To counter negative thinking, we may say something like, *That's not how God sees me, for I am fearfully and wonderfully made. He has plans to prosper and not harm me. I am the apple of His eye. Nothing can separate me from His love. I am His son/daughter.* This is called bringing every thought into the captivity of Christ (2 Corinthians 10:5). From it, we strengthen our faith, which, in turn, gives us the ability to stand on God's promises. For those who are able to keep their eyes focused on God, He promises to keep them in perfect peace, because their minds are steadfast, and they trust in Him (Isaiah 26:3).

Now that the lies of the Enemy have been exposed, we can operate in victory every day while we wait for the move of God. No longer will we be buffeted by the winds of doubt and uncertainty, because we know God is faithful. In retrospect, I learned this lesson at an early age while attending boarding school in Alexandria Virginia. I had a favorite song by James Cleveland that I would sing whenever I felt alone and abandoned, "I Don't Feel No Ways Tired." Unbeknownst to me at that time, I was singing about the unwavering faithfulness of God.

Summary

God has always proved to be faithful in bringing about the destiny of His people. For those who heard His voice and obeyed His commands, they lacked for no good thing. They made a daily decision to operate by faith and not reason. Psalm 18:25 says, *To the faithful you show yourself faithful, to the blameless you show yourself blameless* (NIV).

What are the characteristics of faithful people?

- They follow the leading of the Holy Spirit.

- They choose God's will over their personal desires.

- They pray God's Word and maintain a personal relationship with Him.

- They trust God explicitly.

- More importantly, they proclaim Jesus as Lord and are obedient to the Word.

Unfortunately, this is where a lot of believers miss the mark. While many are willing to make Jesus their Savior, some are reluctant to make Him Lord. In order to be transformed, you must surrender your life to the King of kings and the Lord of lords. In doing so, you may endure a season of challenges which are meant to develop you and not destroy you. Obedience will cause you to sacrifice your personal desires to follow the leading of God. When the transformation process is complete, you can be counted as a vessel of honor, worthy of carrying God's glory on earth. Then God will redeem the dream/vision He gave you.

The person who was once a pleaser of man is now a pleaser of God. The person that was once self-focused is now kingdom-focused. When people look at this person, they see God's glory residing on him/her. That is what Pharaoh and Potiphar saw when they looked at Joseph. They did not see the son of Jacob; they saw a carrier of God's glory on earth. For them, that was the first time they experienced the God of Abraham and Jacob.

Imagine the impact believers would have if they were able to walk with God's glory in the marketplace. Miracles, signs, and wonders would happen every day, and many would come to know Jesus as their Lord and Savior.

If you identified that you are still in the transformation phase, please continue to press forward by faith. Whatever you do, do not abort the process. He has brought you too far to quit now. God is faithful. He is going to help you get through this season. I see tiny clouds on your horizon—the rain is coming.

His divine power has given us everything we need for a godly life through our knowledge of Him who called us by His own glory and goodness.

—2 Peter 1:3 NIV

Reflection Questions

1. In order to see how faithful God is in your life, make a list of all the things He has done for you.

2. How do you start your day? How often do you hear God's instructions for your day?

3. What causes you to look back and long for the comfortable place? Why do you desire the comfortable place more than you desire God's destiny for your life?

4. When you feel like aborting the process, what steps can you take to bring the temptation to quit into the captivity of Christ?

Meditation Scriptures

Galatians 5:22
2 Thessalonians 3:3
Psalm 25:10
Proverbs 16:9
Psalm 36:5
Psalm 43:3
Genesis 18:14

Final Thoughts

THANK YOU FOR investing valuable time reading *The Overflow Blessing.* I pray that this story provides you with insights as you walk out the path to your destiny. Contrary to what the Enemy says, you are right where you need to be in this season. Those setbacks and disappointments have a purpose in God's plan for your life. At the right time, He will open a door and pour out a blessing that you will not have room enough to contain. Therefore, continue pressing forward by faith and standing on the Word of God. Your latter days will be greater!

My desire in writing this book is that every reader be equipped with knowledge to endure the preparation process and receive their overflow blessing. My prayer is that this story encourages those who were feeling faint or on the verge of quitting the process. God has not forgotten about you. He loves you enough to prepared you for an incredible blessing, one that will come upon you suddenly. Fear not, when the door finally opens, you will be ready to receive your *overflow blessing*!

May health and prosperity be upon you and your family,

Shalom Aleichem

ENDNOTES

Chapter 1 The Overflow Blessing
Rick Warren, *The Purpose Driven Life*, (Grand Rapids: Zondervan, 2002)
Chapter 2 God's Love for Us
Stormie Omartian, *Just Enough Light for the Step I'm On: Trusting God in the Tough Times*, (Eugene: Harvest House Publishers, 2008)
Wayne Cordeiro, The Divine Mentor, (Bloomington, Bethany House Publisher, 2007)

Chapter 3 Vision Defines the Destination
Dr. Myles Munroe, *The Principals and Power of Vision*, (New Kensington: Whitaker House,2003). page 25
Dr. Joe Ibojie, *Illustrated Dictionary of Dream Symbols*, (Pescara Italy: DESTINY IMAGE™ EUROPE, 2005), pages 4-5
Stephen R.Covey, *The 7 Habits of Highly Effective People*, (New York, Simon & Schuster, 1990), page 98
John Cook, *The Book of Positive Quotations*, (Minneapolis: Fairview Press, 1993), page 293
Andy Stanley, *Visioneering*, (Colorado Springs, Multonmah Books, 1999)

Chapter 4 Getting into Position

Max Lucado, *Facing Your Giants*, (Nashville: W. Publishing Group, 2006), page 39

John Cook, *The Book of Positive Quotations*, (Minneapolis: Fairview Press, 1993), page 293

Quotesnsayings.net>smight-wigglesworth-quotes/

https://www.thomasedison.com/biography.html

https://www.brainyquotes.com/authors/lao_tzu

Chapter 5 The Preparation

https://www.azquotes.com/author/19080-Rick_Yancey

John Cook, *The Book of Positive Quotations*, (Minneapolis: Fairview Press, 1993), page 118

https://www.azquotes.com/author/16182-Zig_Ziglar/tag/attitude

Chapter 6 The Power of Obedience

Dr. Myles Monroe, *Kingdom Principles*, (Shippensburg: Destiny Image, 2006), page 111-112

https://www.azquotes.com/author/22593-Rod_Parsley

Max Lucado, *Facing Your Giants*, (Nashville: W. Publishing Group, 2006), page 9

Stormie Omartian, *Just Enough Light for the Step I'm On: Trusting God in the Tough Times*, (Eugene: Harvest House Publishers, 2008)

John H. Sammis, *Trust and Obey*, public domain hymn

Chapter 7 Managing the Emotional Roller Coaster

www.abrahamlincolnonline.org/lincoln/speeches/inaug2.htm

John C Maxwell, *The Difference Maker*, (Nashville: Thomas Nelson Inc, 2006), page 118

https://www.azquotes.com/author/64218-Hal_Elrod/tag/gratitude

John Cook, *The Book of Positive Quotations*, (Minneapolis: Fairview Press, 1993), page 364

John Cook, *The Book of Positive Quotations*, (Minneapolis: Fairview Press, 1993), page 366

John Ortberg, *If You Want to Walk on Water, You Have to Get Out of the Boat*, (Grand Rapids: Zondervan, 2001)
John Cook, *The Book of Positive Quotations*, (Minneapolis: Fairview Press, 1993), page 120
https://www.bartleby.com/124/pres49.html

Chapter 8 Divine Elevation and Promotion
Ed Silvoso, *Anointed for Business,* (Bloomington: Chosen Books, 2014), page 59

Chapter 9 Redemption and Restoration
John Cook, *The Book of Positive Quotations*, (Minneapolis: Fairview Press, 1993), page 436

Chapter 10 Surviving the Darkness
https://www.azquotes.com/quote/1033548

Dr. Francis Myles, *Now What?* (Tempe: Order of Melchizedek Holdings LLC, 2014), page 99
https://www.azquotes.com/author/64218-Hal_Elrod/tag/gratitude
https://www.brainyquote.com/authors/melody_beattie

Chapter 11 God is Faithful
https://www.theodysseyonline.com/5-quotes-hard-times

ACKNOWLEGEMENTS

My gratitude extends to all of the people who made this book possible. Thank you Apostle Cassandra Sampson for encouraging me to write this book. You opened doors for me to exercise my spiritual gifts and walk in my calling. You consistently reminded me that I had a story worth telling. You challenged me to go higher on the mountain of God which required a greater level of sacrifice and faith. You lovingly reminded me of God's faithfulness during those difficult days. I am grateful to have you as a spiritual mother.

To my editor, Yvonne Perry, you tutored me on how to write a book. I am grateful for your consistent prodding and words of encouragement. This book exist because of the faith that you had in my vision. The testimony you share based on my incomplete and rambling chapters confirmed that this was my assignment for that season. You patiently coached me to get to the heart of the message. I am blessed to call you friend.

Thanks to my spiritual parents, Dr. Jeffery Chapman and Lady Chapman of Raleigh North Christian Center. Your teachings inspired me to deeper levels of studying God's Word. During the difficult times, your words echoed in my head, "Don't abort the process". I am forever grateful for the seeds of knowledge that you planted in my garden.

Thank you Andrea Murrell for your perspective and editing feedback. Your finishing touches paved the way for final publishing.

Special thanks to my family and friends. You surrounded me with love and support during the most challenging time in my life. More importantly, you spoke life over me while I was going through the transformation process. You believed on the days when my faith could not be found. I honor your faithfulness and your kindness.

I honor my grandparents, Harry Orlo Bright and Vivien King Bright for teaching me the power of persistence. I honor my parents, William Andrew Bright and Bessie Joyce Bright for stressing the importance of education. Their sacrifices created a powerful legacy for our family. To my daughters, Vanessa and Victoria, I love you and am excited to see what God is doing in your lives. Always strive to do your best.

I dedicate this book to back to God who chose me for this assignment. He provided both the revelation and the inspiration for this book. He rewarded my persistent questioning by showing me things hidden in the story of Joseph. He is unwavering in His faithfulness and love for His children.

CPSIA information can be obtained
at www.ICGtesting.com
Printed in the USA
LVHW011514281019
635545LV00002B/371